"Dr. Holzer's work on the Negative is an elegant and transformative read. Situating itself at the crossroads of philosophy and psychoanalysis, Dr. Holzer discusses Negation as not just the engine of destruction and absence but of creativity, the source of conflict and resolution, and even the gateway to transformation and psychic growth - a process of unique emergence through the bold confrontation with it. With breathtaking clarity and intellectual rigor, Dr. Holzer's historical-conceptual journey weaves through Sigmund Freud, Georg Wilhelm Friedrich Hegel, André Green, Laurence Horn, Donald Winnicott, and Wilfred Bion. Age-old Hegelian understandings of forms of Negation are brought into creative focus with psychoanalytic thinkers. This is an invaluable text that clearly illustrates the importance of a relationship between philosophy and psychoanalysis."

Loray Daws, PhD, DPsa, *Psychoanalyst and Clinical Psychologist, Author of* Introduction to the work of Harry J.S. Guntrip.

"In this remarkable textbook, the Negative is restored to its rightful place: not as a void or lack, but as a generative, shaping force at the core of the human psyche. With philosophical and psychoanalytic rigor, this book charts a journey from Hegel to Freud, from Winnicott and Bion to Green, weaving together threads from psychoanalysis, logic, and literature into a rich and lucid tapestry. It offers both scholars and clinicians an indispensable map for navigating the paradoxes of denial, absence, and psychic transformation. A powerful contribution to the field."

Prof. Dana Amir, Ph.D, *Clinical Psychologist, Supervising and Training Analyst, The Israel Psychoanalytic Society and the University of Haifa.*

The Negative

In this comprehensive book, Rakefet Efrat Holzer explores the concept of the negative from psychoanalytic, linguistic and philosophical perspectives.

Efrat Holzer provides a thorough exploration of how negation operates in psychoanalysis and beyond through a systematic examination of its philosophical origins with Georg Wilhelm Friedrich Hegel through Sigmund Freud's foundational insights to André Green's theoretical framework. The book illuminates both destructive and creative dimensions of the negative, exploring concepts such as negative capability, transitional objects and negative hallucination. By weaving together philosophy, psychoanalysis, linguistics, poetry and literature, Efrat Holzer delivers theoretical insights alongside clinical applications, demonstrating how the negative can shape human development, thought processes and therapeutic practice.

This book is essential reading for psychoanalysts, practitioners and trainees in psychiatry, psychotherapy and social work as well as students and researchers interested in psychoanalytic theory.

Rakefet Efrat Holzer is a researcher at the Tel Aviv Institute for Contemporary Psychoanalysis, Israel.

Routledge Introductions to Contemporary Psychoanalysis

Series Editor: Aner Govrin
Executive Editor: Yael Peri Herzovich

Free Association: A Contemporary Introduction
Barnaby B Barratt

Interpretation: A Contemporary Introduction
Aner Govrin

The Negative: A Contemporary Introduction
Rakefet Efrat Holzer

Harry Guntrip: A Contemporary Introduction
Loray Daws

Gender: A Contemporary Introduction
Oren Gozlan

Traumatic Narcissism Theory: A Contemporary Introduction
Daniel Shaw

Philip Bromberg: A Contemporary Introduction
Anthony Bass and Velleda C. Ceccoli

Antisocial Personality Disorder: A Contemporary Introduction
Jessica Yakeley

Pierre Janet: A Contemporary Introduction
Giuseppe Craparo

For more information about this series, please visit:
www.routledge.com/Routledge-Introductions-to-Contemporary-Psychoanalysis/book-series/ICP

The Negative

A Contemporary Introduction

Rakefet Efrat Holzer

Routledge
Taylor & Francis Group
LONDON AND NEW YORK

Designed cover image: © Michal Heiman, Asylum 1855–2020,
The Sleeper (video, psychoanalytic sofa and Plate 34), exhibition
view, Herzliya Museum of Contemporary Art, 2017

First published 2026
by Routledge
4 Park Square, Milton Park, Abingdon, Oxon OX14 4RN

and by Routledge
605 Third Avenue, New York, NY 10158

*Routledge is an imprint of the Taylor & Francis Group, an informa
business*

British Library Cataloguing-in-Publication Data
A catalogue record for this book is available from the British
Library

ISBN: 978-1-032-40386-1 (hbk)
ISBN: 978-1-032-40279-6 (pbk)
ISBN: 978-1-003-35285-3 (ebk)

DOI: 10.4324/9781003352853

Typeset in Times New Roman
by Taylor & Francis Books

Contents

Series Editor's Preface

Routledge Introductions to Contemporary Psychoanalysis is one of the most prominent psychoanalytic publishing ventures of our day. The series' aim is to become an encyclopedia of psychoanalysis, with each entry given its own book.

This comprehensive series illuminates the intricate landscape of psychoanalytic theory and practice. In this collection of concise yet illuminating volumes, we delve into the influential figures, groundbreaking concepts, and transformative theories that shape the contemporary psychoanalytic landscape.

At the heart of each volume lies a commitment to clarity, accessibility, and depth. Our expert authors, renowned scholars and practitioners in their respective fields, guide readers through the complexities of psychoanalytic thought with precision and enthusiasm. Whether you are a seasoned psychoanalyst, a student eager to explore the field, or a curious reader seeking insight into the human psyche, our series offers a wealth of knowledge and insight.

Each volume serves as a gateway into a specific aspect of psychoanalytic theory and practice. From the pioneering works of Sigmund Freud to the innovative contributions of modern theorists such as Antonino Ferro and Michal Eigen, our series covers a diverse range of topics, including seminal figures, key concepts, and emerging trends. Whether you are interested in classical psychoanalysis, object relations theory, or the intersection of neuroscience and psychoanalysis, you will find a wealth of resources within our collection.

One of the hallmarks of our series is its interdisciplinary approach. While rooted in psychoanalytic theory, our volumes draw upon insights from psychology, philosophy, sociology, and other disciplines to offer a holistic understanding of the human mind and its complexities.

Each volume in the series is crafted with the reader in mind, balancing scholarly rigor with engaging prose. Whether you are embarking on your journey into psychoanalysis or seeking to deepen your understanding of specific topics, our series provides a clear and comprehensive roadmap.

Moreover, our series is committed to fostering dialogue and debate within the psychoanalytic community. Each volume invites readers to critically engage with the material, encouraging reflection, discussion, and further exploration.

We invite you to join us on this journey of discovery as we explore the ever-evolving landscape of psychoanalysis.

Aner Govrin

Introduction

The poets and philosophers before me discovered the unconscious;
  what I discovered was the scientific method by which the unconscious
  can be studied.
(Freud, The Interpretation of Dreams SE Vol. 4, 86)

Negation is present in every human language yet absent from animal communication – facts that highlight its status as a *sine qua non* of the human form of life. It has long fascinated philosophers, linguists, and psychoanalysts, from Plato and Hegel to Freud, Green, and contemporary thinkers, due to its profound implications for the human mind, language, and identity, as well as its uniquely human capacities, such as denial, resistance, contradiction, and irony. Negation is everywhere. It is the force that makes our thoughts possible, propels our desires, shapes our identities, buries our hopes, and creates the springboard for our self-transcendence. From the child's first "no" to the adult's silent suppression of uncomfortable truths, negation is deeply woven into the fabric of our mental and emotional lives. At its core, logical and linguistic entity – ingrained, versatile, and multi-faceted, it has the capacity to take on various forms and adapt to diverse contexts and fields across human culture. It is the engine of destruction but also of creativity, the source of conflict and resolution, and the gateway to transformation and psychic growth. The Negative, thus, is not merely about what is absent or

DOI: 10.4324/9781003352853-1

denied – it is about what emerges through the bold confrontation or "tarrying" with it.

The present research situates itself at the crossroads of philosophy and psychoanalysis. It investigates the psychoanalytic concept of the Negative by first examining its logical and philosophical origins, and then tracing its intellectual evolution within psychoanalysis, constructing a narrative that uncovers the theoretical and clinical meanings of the concept. The rationale for this approach lies in the recognition that psychoanalytic concepts often draw extensively from earlier philosophical thought. Engaging with philosophical reflections on negation and the Negative thus lays the groundwork for a deeper, more nuanced understanding of their significance within psychoanalytic theory and practice. Additionally, following Freud's poignant observation that wherever a psychoanalyst reaches, a poet has already been there, this study also incorporates literary works, weaving them into the discussion where their unique contributions can enrich the discussion.

The historical-conceptual journey proposed in this book begins with Freud's thinking and concludes with André Green's, retracing the path that led to Green's endpoint. In other words, Green's concept of the Negative is treated as a culmination, an apex shaped by various contributions over time, and while these contributions are by no means less significant, this apex's development serves as the central narrative thread of the journey presented here. A preliminary glance at this narrative reveals that Green adopted the philosopher J. W. F. Hegel's idea of "The Work of the Negative" as the skeleton of the Negative, to which he added Freudian flesh, clothed it with the creative contributions of later analysts – most notably Winnicott and Bion – and ultimately shaped it into a dynamic and multidimensional construct – an intricate framework that transcends being merely an adjective (negative X) to become a noun (the Negative), denoting a central organizing principle within psychoanalytic theory and practice.

A conceptual clarification is necessary at the outset: a significant portion of this book focuses on the concept of "negation". This is because negation serves as both the foundation and origin of the concept of the Negative in psychoanalysis, historically as well as conceptually and theoretically. And while the Negative can be understood as an overarching psycho-analytic concept that incorporates negation, negation essentially plays a central role within it. Being more fundamental and widespread than the concept of the Negative, negation has been studied more extensively in both philosophy and psychoanalysis, and this book builds upon these studies.

Negation, according to philosopher and logician Laurence Horn, is a "tantalizing" and elusive concept. The following anec-dote illustrates its abstruseness. During one of his lectures, John Austin, one of the most influential philosophers of language in the twentieth century, argued that in all natural languages known to him, a double negation creates an affirmation. Conversely, Austin claimed, he was unaware of any natural language in which a double affirmation produces a negation. "Yes, yes", he stated, will always mean "yes". To this, the philosopher Sidney Morgenbesser, known for his sharp and sardonic wit, ironically replied: "Yeah, yeah." Paradoxically, as this anecdote implies, while the meaning of negation as a logical or linguistic operation – or at least the use of it – is intuitive to any speaker of a language, it is revealed as a complex and slippery concept that defies definitive definition. It possesses an almost diabolical quality, capable of complicating matters just as much as it can confuse the listener or reader (e.g., "It is not uncommon for individuals to not avoid situations where they might not be unable to express dissatisfaction"). The rela-tionship between negation and affirmation is equally unsettled. Moreover, using negation to describe specific material, physical, or mental processes or actions – such as in philosophy and psycho-analysis – is intuitive yet difficult to explain. In a sense, its use in these contexts might be considered metaphorical. This raises challenging questions: What are the central properties of negation that allow for its transfer from the logical or linguistic domains to other fields, such as psychoanalysis? What transforms certain somatic or mental processes or actions into forms of negation? Why, for instance, does Hegel describe the erosion of a stone by water, the devouring of a deer by a lioness, or the production of knowledge by a subject as acts of negation? Why does Freud so clearly identify phenomena such as the inhibition of impulses or the repression of representations as forms of negation?

Negation is a plastic phenomenon. Primarily signifying a *reversal* or *inversion* – an action through which something becomes the *opposite* of what it was – the act of saying (or signaling) "no" embodies rejection, refusal, denial, cancellation, elimination, and more. Furthermore, ontologically, it can deny the existence of something, whether present or absent ("This pen does not exist" or "There is no giraffe in this room") and produces absence or nothingness by negating what exists. And yet, negation is two-faced. Acts of negation can be destructive or constructive, harmful or beneficial. For example, the denial of an unpleasant perception may serve as a useful defense mechanism, but when taken to an extreme, it can lead to psychosis. This suggests that negation is not inherently value-laden but *value-free*: negative actions or their consequences are not intrinsically bad, just as positive, affirmative deeds and processes are not necessarily good. Negation also possesses a unique logical property on which the anecdote above hinges: its repeated application is governed by the "law of double negation", which states that the double negation of a proposition is equivalent to the proposition itself. In other words, when negation is applied to an already negated proposition, the effect of the first negation is cancelled – essentially, "no no" means "yes." This principle finds significant application in psychoanalysis. Freud, for example, characterizes repression as a negative process that transforms conscious material into its opposite – that is, unconscious material. However, when repression is itself negated (as in Freud's well-known example, when the patient declares, "it is not my mother"), the repression is cancelled; the unconscious material is released and, to some extent, becomes conscious. This interplay of negation, its intricacies, dual nature, immense powers, and transformative potential is explored in depth throughout the book.

The first chapter lays the foundation by examining the philosophical – metaphysical and logical – roots of negation, tracing its historical and conceptual evolution while addressing the perennial challenges thinkers have faced in defining its bounds. While negation is an inherent part of human rationality and communication – something even a child intuitively grasps – the intellectual attempts to demarcate its meaning remain fraught with complexity. These challenges, however, are not futile; they offer profound insights into the powers and functions of negation in logic, language, and metaphysics, insights that set the stage for understanding its operation in psychoanalysis.

The second chapter dives into the philosophy of G. W. F. Hegel, who coined the phrase "The Work of the Negative", a central tenet of his dialectical philosophy. Negation is deeply embedded in the very fabric of Hegel's thought, shaping both his methodology and his themes. Hegel's systematic and inventive use of negation makes his philosophy especially valuable for illuminating its versatile and multifaceted functions. Furthermore, Hegel's influence on Western thought (whether through direct adoption or through criticism of his system) is so profound that it permeates modern discourse, often shaping the thinking of those who reflect on negation, whether consciously or not. This chapter highlights how Hegel's dialectical approach and his emphasis on the transformative power of the negative provide a unique lens for understanding its role in human development, language, and thought.

The psychoanalytic part of the book begins in Chapter 3 with Freud, whose sensitivity to negation is evident from the very inception of his work. In *The Interpretation of Dreams* (1900), Freud proposed the provocative idea that negation is absent from the unconscious. This observation is explored in the chapter's first section, offering a glimpse into the non-classical, negation-less logic of the unconscious and its unique rules. The second section provides a historical perspective on the diverse mental mechanisms and processes Freud identified as "negative", exploring their evolutionary relationships. Finally, the chapter includes a close reading of Freud's seminal essay "Negation" (1925), where he explicitly outlines his views on negation's clinical use, its archaic roots, and its connection to the drives.

Chapters 4 and 5 focus on the contributions of Donald Winnicott and Wilfred Bion, respectively. While neither explicitly formulated a concept of the Negative, their works illuminate aspects of it in profound ways. Both psychoanalysts explore the dual nature of the negative – its constructive and destructive faces. Winnicott examines the creative potential of the negative through the transitional object and transitional space, while Bion introduces the concept of "negative capability". For both, the child's experience of the absence of the primary object and their ability to cope with it are pivotal moments, dividing development from disaster. Winnicott frames this divide in terms of the duration of the mother's absence, while Bion emphasizes the innate and acquired capacity to endure frustration. The destructive side of the negative is also explored. Winnicott's clinical case involving a patient preoccupied with the "negative side of relationships" provides a striking example of the pathological aspects of the negative. Bion's exploration of the destructive pole of the negative is analyzed through concepts such as "no-thing" versus "nothing", the "minus" (particularly –K), and the "negative power".

Chapter 6 turns to André Green, whose concept of the Negative stands as the culmination of this intellectual journey. Building on the work of his predecessors, Green shaped the concept into a complex framework with theoretical and clinical dimensions. The chapter begins by exploring the various meanings of "The Work of the Negative" in Green's thought, followed by an analysis of the theoretical backdrop underpinning his ideas. Green, like Winnicott and Bion, identifies a dividing line between the developmental and pathological. His concept of the "framing structure" serves to demonstrate this divide. The chapter then delves into Green's innovative contributions to the study of the Negative, examining concepts such as "disobjectalization", "negative hallucination", the "blank series", and "negative narcissism", the latter analyzed through a reference to Herman Melville's *Bartleby, the Scrivener*. These inventive yet elusive ideas are unpacked and made accessible. The chapter concludes by outlining some of Green's clinical reflections.

This book embarks on a journey to provide a concise yet in-depth examination of the concept of the Negative – its meanings, manifestations, and evolution within psychoanalysis – rooted in philosophical knowledge. Along this journey, readers are invited to explore both the devastating and elevating dimensions of the Negative, as well as its profound and transformative role in shaping human thought, development, and well-being – or the consequences of its failure to do so.

Chapter 1

The Logic of Negation[1]

"Negation", as the prominent logician Laurence Horn cautions, "is to the linguist and linguistic philosopher as fruit to Tantalus: waving seductively, alluringly palpable, yet just out of reach, within the grasp only to escape once more" (Horn 2001, xiv). The history of negation is an ongoing and polemical dialogue among thinkers, saturated with unresolved controversies. Horn, whose monumental work *A Natural History of Negation* (2001) heavily informs this chapter, demonstrates that while negation is a fundamental and indispensable element in both classical and non-classical logics, as well as in all natural languages, it has eluded consensus regarding its definition, logical status, meaning, function, and scope of applicability. Despite centuries of inquiry by philosophers, logicians, and linguists, even basic questions such as "What is a negative proposition?" remain unsettled (Heinemann 1944, 135 in Horn 2001, 1).

This lack of resolution, however, should not lead us to dismiss the history of the study of negation as fruitless or irrelevant. On the contrary, the efforts to define and understand negation have laid the groundwork for a rich intellectual tradition. The ancient Greeks, for instance, provided foundational definitions, distinctions, and logical laws that have served as common ground or productive points of contention for centuries. Building on this fertile intellectual tradition, generations of thinkers have developed a rich – albeit non-unified – discussion, a taste of which I will present below. In this chapter, I will first outline the ancient

DOI: 10.4324/9781003352853-2

cornerstones of the logic of negation and then explore historically pivotal debates, shedding light on the complexities of the concept.

Negation, though elusive and resistant to a widely accepted definition, is intuitively understood by anyone who uses language. Nevertheless, some conventions can be safely proposed. From a logical perspective, negation is a connective that reverses the truth value of a proposition: when applied to a true statement, it renders it false, and vice versa. Linguistically, negation is an operation that alters a sentence's meaning to express its opposite (e.g., "Jerusalem is the capital of Israel" is a true proposition, the negation of which expresses the opposite and renders it false).

Negation in Ontology

Historically, negation first emerged in philosophical thought within an *ontological* context, as part of the inquiry into *what exists in the world*. Before even thinking about scrutinizing negation as a linguistic or logical operation, early thinkers focused on metaphysical questions about the negation of being, or "not-being" and "nothingness" – as opposed to "being". One of the earliest and most influential contributions to this topic came from Parmenides of Elea, a pre-Socratic philosopher of the early fifth century BC.

In his famous poem *On Nature*, Parmenides introduces a distinctive view on the nature of being and non-being:

Come now, I will tell thee – and do thou hearken to my saying and carry it away – the only two ways of search that can be thought of. The first, namely, that It is, and that it is impossible for anything not to be, is the way of conviction, for truth is its companion. The other, namely, that It is not, and that something must needs not be, – that, I tell thee, is a wholly untrustworthy path. For you cannot know what is not – that is impossible – nor utter it…Parmenides immediately dismisses the second way of inquiry, which concerns "what is not", as invalid. He insists that only "what is" can be the subject of inquiry and conviction, while "what is not" is unintelligible and inexpressible. He elaborates further:

It needs must be that what can be thought and spoken of *is*; for it is possible for it to be, and it is not possible for what is nothing to be. This is what I bid thee ponder.

(Translated by John Burnet, 1892)

Parmenides rejects the existence of non-being, asserting that only being exists. Non-being, or nothingness, is necessarily nonexistent and cannot be known or even thought. Attempting to think of non being, he argues, transforms it into something – it ceases to be nothing and becomes an object for thought – something that exists. To assert that non-being *is*, or that nothing exists, is a paradox. As he famously states: "For this shall never be proved, that the things that are not are" For Parmenides, pursuing this line of inquiry leads to a contradiction, which reason cannot tolerate. Thus, he concludes that "what is, is" and "what is not, is not".

Parmenides grounds his philosophy firmly in reason, rejecting knowledge derived from the senses, which he deems deceptive and unreliable. For example, while the senses might perceive the sun as smaller than a hand, reason reveals the truth that the sun is far larger than the Earth, appearing small only because of its immense distance. Reality, for Parmenides, is hidden from the senses and accessible only through the rigorous application of reason.

This reasoning leads Parmenides to a monistic metaphysics, in which everything is unified in a static, eternal One. In the Parmenidean world, plurality, creation, annihilation, change, movement, and time are impossible because they all rely on the concept of nothingness, which he rejects. For instance, creation implies that something comes into being from nothing, while annihilation implies that something ceases to exist and becomes nothing. Change, similarly, involves something becoming other than itself – what it was not. For example, when an apple changes color from green to red, redness, which was previously absent (non-being), comes into being, while greenness, which was present, ceases to exist. Without the concept of nothingness, such transformations are inconceivable. Movement, as a form of change, is similarly dismissed, and without movement, time itself becomes unthinkable. Thus, Parmenides dismisses the entire phenomenal world of sensory experience, with its transient and shifting plurality, as illusory and false.

Plato (427–347 BC) addresses the concept of negation in his dialogue *The Sophist*. The main interlocutor, the Eleatic Stranger – a student of Parmenides – critically engages with his master's philosophy and transcends it. In this dialogue, Plato contests Parmenides' conclusion that non-being cannot exist and, therefore, cannot be known or spoken of. He does so by *redefining the very meaning of negation*: rather than signifying opposition, it signifies *difference*. For Plato, "not A" does not necessarily mean the opposite of A, nor does it imply that A does not exist. Instead, it means that A is something *other* than what it positively is. For instance, Plato asks: when we say "not great", do we necessarily mean "little"? Or could it mean something like "average in size"?

This redefinition entails that *negation no longer nullifies what it negates*. The radical implication of this claim is that when something is negated, it nevertheless retains a form of being. "Not-great" is as much a part of being as "great". By extension, "not-being" also participates in the class of "being". It is a form of being that is different from being but is not equivalent to nothing. As the Stranger says: "May I not say with confidence that not-being has an assured existence, and a nature of its own?" (Plato 2013, 258). Plato thus argues that non-being exists, successfully avoiding the contradiction that Parmenides feared: "Let not any one say, then, that while affirming the opposition of not-being to being, we still assert the being of not-being; for as to whether there is an opposite of being, to that inquiry we have long said good-bye" (258–259).

That said, Plato does not directly resolve the problem – or paradox – of nothingness. Instead, he circumvents it by redefining negation in *positive* terms of difference or otherness. In doing so, Plato effectively abandons negation's traditional notion of opposition for one of absolute positivity. This raises the question of whether Plato's theory still qualifies as a theory of negation. According to Eric Toms, the problem with Plato's approach is that it sacrifices negation's principal trait: its power of *exclusion*.

As Toms writes, "[T]he fact taking the place of the negative fact has still to exclude from existence the opposite positive fact" (Toms 1972, 8, in Horn 2001, 51). By omitting this exclusionary aspect, Plato risks collapsing back into the Parmenidean One, where differentiation between things – and thus plurality – becomes impossible.

Plato's exploration of negation in *The Sophist* remains firmly rooted in ontology, focusing on the question of being and non-being. However, his inquiry also ventures into the realm of language, examining the meaning and function of negation as a component of propositions. In this sense, Plato pioneers a linguistic approach to negation, laying the groundwork for his pupil Aristotle, who takes a significant leap forward by formalizing negation in strictly logical terms.

Before turning to Aristotle, it is worth reflecting on why Plato redefines negation, abandoning its oppositional or negative aspect in favor of difference. The answer lies in the inherent complexity of negative propositions, which tend to be problematic, confusing, and even paradoxical, especially when compared to affirmative propositions. This difficulty has been noted by philosophers from Parmenides to Bertrand Russell and beyond. As Horn (2001) observes, negative propositions often appear unintelligible or self-contradictory, as Parmenides' argument demonstrates. Modern examples, such as "This assertion is not true" or "This chair does not exist", similarly reveal the perplexities of negation (Horn 2001, xiv). The confusion becomes even more acute when dealing with multiple negations. For instance, consider the statement, "It is not a mistake to say that when double negation is not used, assertions are not confusing". Such a statement demonstrates the inherent difficulty of negation, which can obscure meaning rather than clarify it.

Moreover, negative propositions are often less specific and less informative than affirmatives. Aristotle points out: "We say that he who knows that the thing is something has understanding to a higher degree than he who knows that it is not something" (Aristotle, *Metaphysics*, 996b14–16 in Horn 2001, 47). For example, if we wish to know the color of Michael's hat, the statement "Michael's hat is not red" provides far less information than

"Michael's hat is blue". This lack of specificity and informativeness, among other shortcomings, makes negation particularly challenging for philosophers, especially those like Plato, for whom language is an essential tool of inquiry.

Negation in Logic

Aristotle was the first philosopher to abstract negation from its ontological roots and systematically theorize it in formal, logical, and linguistic terms. His ideas on this topic, scattered across several works, became the foundation of classical logic. Even 2,500 years later, Aristotle's insights into negation remain as relevant as ever, providing the bedrock of Western rational thought and serving as both a foundation and a point of contention for later logicians who developed non-classical logics. In this section, I will focus on Aristotle's most significant observations and formulations regarding negation – those that contribute to a concise understanding of classical logic and are most relevant to the psychoanalytic discussion central to this book.

At the heart of Aristotle's logic lies the distinction between contraries (or oppositions) and contradictions. This distinction is based on two key criteria: (A) Oppositions pertain to concepts, while contradictions refer to propositions. Aristotle defines contradiction as a relation in which "statements are opposed to each other as affirmation and negation" (Aristotle, *Categories*, 13b2–3, in Horn 2001, 8). A contradiction consists of two propositions connected by the conjunction "and", where one affirms what the other denies (e.g., "Michael's hat is red and Michael's hat is not red"). Propositions represent ideas due to including both a subject and a predicate (property). By contrast, oppositions, such as "good and bad" or "happy and unhappy", do not constitute contradictions for a reason specified in the next criterion. (B) In a contradiction, one proposition must be true, and the other false (Horn 2001, 8). One proposition affirms a fact about the world, which the other denies. The proposition that corresponds to the fact is true, while the other is necessarily false. Oppositions, by contrast, are not concerned with truth or falsehood, as single terms do not correspond to facts about the world.

Based on these distinctions, Aristotle formulated two fundamental laws of classical logic: the "law of contradiction" (also named the "law of non-contradiction") and the "law of excluded middle". These laws, which Aristotle regarded as axiomatic (from the Greek for "that which commends itself as evident"), form the keystones of classical logic. As Aristotle explains in *Metaphysics* (996b 18–30), these laws are part of "the common doctrines from which all men prove something" (Horn 2001, 18). In other words, they are indispensable conditions for the creation of coherent, intelligible meaning and for valid reasoning.

Aristotle articulated two versions of the "law of contradiction". The first, applying to the *subject* of a proposition, states: "It is impossible to be and not to be at the same time." The second, applying to the *predicate* of a subject states: "The same thing cannot at the same time both belong and not belong to the same object and in the same respect" (Aristotle, *Metaphysics*, 1005b 19–23, in Horn 2001, 18). Violations of these laws result in irrational propositions. For example, the first version is violated by statements like "The Pantheon exists and the Pantheon does not exist", while the second is violated by "Achilles is brave and Achilles is not brave".

The "law of excluded middle" complements these rules by asserting that "In every case we must either affirm or deny" (Aristotle, *Metaphysics*, 1005b 19–23 in Horn 2001, 19). This means that in the case of contradictory propositions, if one is true, the other must necessarily be false. In other words, a proposition must either be true or false, with no third option or "middle" term. For example, Achilles must either be brave or not brave; no intermediate state exists. This law reinforces the binary structure of classical logic, though the explicit formulation of "either-or" propositions came later.

Aristotle's logic, as Horn explains, is a *logic of terms*, where negation is *internal* to the proposition, which must be categorical – that is, it "consists of something (the subject) about which something (the predicate) is affirmed or denied" (Horn 2001, 14). A categorical proposition contains only one predicate, so negation occurs only *once* (22). Later, the Stoics introduced *external* negation, allowing statements like "Not: it is raining" (meaning

"It is not the case that it is raining") and multiple negations. This led to the "law of double negation", which asserts that negating a negation equals affirmation, as Alexander of Aphrodisias noted: "Not: not: it is raining" is essentially the same as "It is raining" (Mates 1953, 126, in Horn 2001, 22). Thinkers like Hegel later rejected this position. With the Stoics, this brief outline of negation's history in classical philosophy and logic comes to an end. However, the questions and topics raised by Aristotle and his successors have continued to fuel lively debates to this day. A closer examination of these debates provides valuable insights into the nature of negation. Hence, I will focus on three fundamental classical and post-classical controversies.

Three Unresolved Controversies

The first question to be examined is: *Is there symmetry or asymmetry between affirmative and negative propositions?* Every philosopher, logician, or linguist who has engaged with the concept of negation has taken a stance on this issue, although some (such as Aristotle and Russell) can be seen as supporting both sides to varying degrees. The first explicit articulation of the asymmetric position came from the eighth-century Indian philosopher and logician Śaṅkara, who argued that the negative is either dependent on the positive or else insignificant (Horn 2001, 64). Proponents of this view generally agree that "*every negative statement presupposes a corresponding affirmative [...] but not vice versa*" (Horn 2001, 3, emphasis added); for example, the statement "Greece does not lie by the sea" presupposes and negates the statement "Greece lies by the sea". Thus, negative claims are conceived as *second-order propositions.*

Advocates of the asymmetric position argue that negative statements are secondary and inferior to affirmative ones across logical, ontological, epistemological, and psychological dimensions. Ontologically, Plato in *The Sophist* notes that for any subject, only a finite number of predicates can be affirmed, while an infinite number can be denied (Plato, *The Sophist*, 256E, in Horn 2001, 60). For example, an apple may be round and red, but it is not countless other shapes or colors. Aristotle echoes this asymmetry both epistemologically and ontologically, claiming that "The affirmative proposition is prior to and is better known than the negative (since affirmation explains denial just as being is prior to not-being)" (Aristotle, *Posterior Analytics*, 86b33–36, in Horn 2001, 47). Similarly, Aquinas places being above non-being, asserting that a "to be" proposition is prior to a "not to be" proposition, just as owning something is prior to being deprived of it (Aristotle, *De Interpretatione*, Book 1, Lesson 13, in Horn 2001, 47). For Aquinas, "negative statements are about positive statements, while affirmatives are directly about the world" (Horn 2001, 3). For instance, "The apple is not red" *presupposes* and denies the positive statement "The apple is red", while the latter statement refers to reality itself (Meyer 1944, 358). In this sense, the positive serves as the foundation for the negative, reinforcing Aquinas's claim that being (positive) is ontologically prior to non-being (negative).

Epistemologically, Aristotle and Aquinas argue for the primacy of affirmation over negation. Aquinas states that "with respect to thought, the affirmative enunciation, which signifies composition by the intellect, is prior to the negative, which signifies division" (Aristotle, *De Interpretatione*, Book 1, Lesson 13, in Horn 2001, 47). Freud's psychoanalytic theory, as we shall see in Chapter 3, draws deeply on this psychological asymmetry, linking affirmation with unity and negation to processes of division and the disintegration. Kant, in the eighteenth century, supports Aristotle's epistemological position by asserting that negative judgments are not regarded as highly valuable: "[T]hey are regarded rather as the jealous enemies of our unceasing endeavour to extend our knowledge. […] In respect to the content of our knowledge, […], the task peculiar to negative judgments is that of rejecting error" (Kant 1964, 574, A709/B737, in Horn 2001, 61). In other words, negative judgments are limited in their contribution to knowledge, serving primarily to exclude falsehoods rather than to generate new insights.

Psychologically, asymmetricalists argue that negative judgments are inherently subjective. Henri Bergson, one of the key proponents of this view, asserts that "negation is only an attitude taken by the mind toward an eventual affirmation" (Bergson 1911, 287–

288, in Horn 2001, 62). He further explains that "negation inherently involves 'the disappointment of a real or possible expectation'" (62). For Bergson, denial presupposes an affirmative judgment, as there is no reason to deny something that has not first been affirmed. This view is exemplified by Thomas Givón, a mid-twentieth-century linguist, who argues that a statement like "My wife is not pregnant" only becomes meaningful when there is some underlying context or reason to deny the affirmative counterpart (Horn 2001, 72).

In contrast, the *symmetrical position* argues that affirmation and negation are equally fundamental and mutually implicating. This view is supported by various positivist philosophers and can also be traced back to the ancient Greeks. Aristotle appears to endorse a symmetrical stance when he states: "Every affirmation has a corresponding negation" (Aristotle, *Prior Analytics*, 51b35, in Horn 2001, 48). However, asymmetricalists note that Aristotle did not explicitly formulate the reverse claim – that is, that every negation has a corresponding affirmation (48). The Neoplatonist philosopher Porphyry also supports the symmetrical perspective, arguing that because both affirmation and denial can be either true or false, there is no substantial asymmetry between them (Bosley 1975, 7, in Horn 2001, 47). Similarly, Gottlob Frege, the father of analytic philosophy, supports symmetry by claiming that "For every thought there is a contradictory thought" (Frege 1919, 131, in Horn 2001, 48). Alfred J. Ayer, a twentieth-century philosopher of language, acknowledges that negative statements are often – perhaps even most commonly – "used to deny a previous suggestion". However, Ayer questions why it should be more plausible to claim that the assertion "It is not raining" presupposes a suggestion that it is raining than to claim that the assertion "It is raining" presupposes a suggestion that it is not (Ayer [1952] 1963, 39, in Horn 2001, 76). Ayer views affirmation and negation as mutually implicating, writing: "To say what things are not is itself a way of saying what they are" just as much as the reverse (76).

The second major question concerning negation that has preoccupied post-classical thinkers is: *Are there negative facts?* This question is aptly represented in the "paradox of negative judgment": "If a positive statement refers or corresponds to a positive fact, to what does a negative statement refer or correspond?" (Horn 2001, 3). This paradox arises from the correspondence theory of truth, which holds that a proposition is true only if it corresponds to an equivalent fact in the world. For instance, the proposition "The cat is on the mat" is true if, and only if, there is indeed a cat on the mat. However, applying this theory to false or negative propositions raises significant challenges. Statements such as "John is not in the room" or "There is no giraffe in this class" prompt the question: "What objective facts, if any, serve as their truth-makers?" (Oaklander and Miracchi 1980, 435). In the absence of a corresponding positive fact, it becomes unclear how negative statements can be grounded in reality. This issue highlights the difficulty of reconciling negative propositions with a correspondence-based framework of truth and continues to fuel debates about the nature of negation and its relationship to reality. Ludwig Wittgenstein rejects the notion of negative facts, viewing negation as a purely logical operator without any corresponding entity in the world. In his perspective, negation holds no "ontological significance" (Horn 2001, 441). Most contemporary philosophers align with Wittgenstein's stance, treating negation as a formal operation rather than something that corresponds to an objective aspect of reality.

However, Bertrand Russell stands as a notable exception. Russell recalls that when he first challenged Wittgenstein's position before students at Harvard, "it nearly produced a riot". He acknowledges the intuitive discomfort with negative facts: "One has a certain repugnance to negative facts. […] You have a feeling that there are only positive facts, and that negative propositions have somehow or other got to be expressions of positive facts" (Russell 2010, 42). Nevertheless, Russell argues that accepting negative facts is simpler and more consistent than attempting to reduce them to positive ones. He contends that the world is best described by all propositions that capture the totality of facts, whether positive or negative (Dukelow 1976, 8). As Russell puts it, "It is a real question whether in a complete description of the world you would have to mention negative facts or not" (Russell 2010, 46). Ultimately, Russell concludes that accepting negative facts as genuine facts is more parsimonious: "It is simpler to take negative facts as facts, to assume that 'Socrates is not alive' is really an objective fact in the same sense in which 'Socrates is human' is a fact" (45).

The third key question in the post-Classical debate on negation is: *What is a negative proposition?* Defining and distinguishing negative propositions has proven complex. The Stoics narrowly defined negative propositions as those *beginning* with a negative word, classifying statements like "Pain is not good" as affirmative since they expressed a positive claim about what is pain. In contrast, during the Classical and Medieval periods, any statement with "not" in the predicate, such as "Pain is not good" or "The soul is not mortal", was considered negative. Kant refined this further, accepting "The soul is not mortal" as negative but arguing that "The soul is immortal" was affirmative, as it attributes a property (albeit a negative one) to the soul rather than *denying* one.

This debate about the nature of negative propositions led Josiah Royce, a twentieth-century idealist philosopher, to make a bold assertion: he claimed that a coherent class of negative propositions is practically impossible to define. Royce argued that "every denial is *ipso facto* an affirmation, and vice versa, since 'to affirm is to deny the contradictory of whatever one affirms'" (Royce 1917, 265–266, in Horn 2001, 33). Frege reinforced Royce's view by stating: "A negation may occur anywhere in a sentence without making the thought indubitably negative" (Frege 1919, 125, in Horn 2001, 33). Through these critiques, Royce and Frege problematized the very distinction between affirmative and negative propositions, suggesting that the boundary between the two is far less clear than traditionally assumed.

The elusive and confusingly paradoxical nature of negation is aptly captured by the poet H. Mearns (1899) in his famous verse:

> Yesterday upon the stair
> I met a man who wasn't there
> He wasn't there again today
> I wish, I wish he'd go away.

As Horn summarizes, the history of this debate has failed to produce a universally accepted definition of negative propositions. No clear criteria have been established to definitively determine which statements belong to this category, leaving the concept of negation an unresolved issue in philosophical and logical discourse. Overall, negation reveals itself as a conundrum that arises largely from its inherently confounding nature, as illustrated above. It is precisely this intricate quality that resonates within the discourse of psychoanalysis, as we will explore in the subsequent chapters.

Note

1 I am grateful to Dr. Amit Saad for reading this chapter and providing insightful comments.

Recommended Reading

Déprez, Viviane, and M. Teresa Espinal, eds. 2020. *The Oxford Handbook of Negation*. Oxford: Oxford University Press.

Horn, Laurence R. 2001. *A Natural History of Negation*. Stanford, CA: CSLI Publications, Leland Stanford Junior University.

Speranza, J. L., and Laurence R. Horn, 2010. "A Brief History of Negation", *Journal of Applied Logic* 8 (3): 277–301.

Reference List

Dukelow, Owen W. 1976. "The Problem of Negative Facts in Russell's Logical Atomism". *The Southwestern Journal of Philosophy* 7 (1): 7–13.

Horn, Laurence R. 2001. *A Natural History of Negation*. Stanford, CA: CSLI Publications, Leland Stanford Junior University.

Mearns, Hughes. 1899. "Antigonish". *Academy of American Poets.* https://poets.org/poem/antigonish-i-met-man-who-wasnt-there.

Meyer, Hans. 1944. *The Philosophy of St. Thomas Aquinas*. Translated by Frederic Eckhoff. St. Louis and London: B. Herder Book Co.

Oaklander, L. Nathan, and Lisa Miracchi. 1980. "Russell, Negative Facts, and Ontology". *Philosophy of Science* 47 (3): 434–455.

Parmenides. 1892. *On Nature*. Translated by John Burnet. http://philoc
tetes.free.fr/parmenidesunicode.htm.

Plato. 2013. *The Sophist*. Translated by Benjamin Jowett. Project Gutenberg. www.gutenberg.org/files/1735/1735-h/1735-h.htm.

Russell, Bertrand. [1972] 2010. *The Philosophy of Logical Atomism*.
London and New York: Routledge.

Chapter 2

Hegel
A Philosophy of Negativity

Georg Wilhelm Friedrich Hegel (1770–1831), a German philosopher and central figure in German Idealism, has profoundly influenced a wide range of philosophical traditions (e.g., Marxism, Existentialism, Pragmatism) and disciplines (e.g., metaphysics, political philosophy, aesthetics). Thinkers such as Karl Marx, Søren Kierkegaard, Friedrich Nietzsche, Martin Heidegger, and Jean-Paul Sartre grappled with his ideas, often critically. As Maurice Merleau-Ponty observed, "[Hegel's] successors placed more emphasis on what they rejected of his heritage than on what they owe to him" (Rockmore 2010). Nevertheless, many of the major philosophical ideas of the past century can trace their origins back to Hegel's work.

Hegel's philosophy, which Jean Hyppolite (1979) described as a "philosophy of negation and negativity", is pivotal to understanding the role of negation in Western thought and psychoanalysis. His system is ambitious, aiming to provide a comprehensive explanation of reality through a single organizing principle. However, it is notoriously complex, due to three primary factors: his dense and often cryptic writing style, his rigid yet opaque methodology, and the vast scope of his engagement with philosophical, cultural, and historical ideas. As a result, Hegel's work has been interpreted in widely divergent – and sometimes contradictory – ways, encompassing religious and secular, idealist and social readings, among others. My own discussion of Hegel's concept of negativity will necessarily be brief and narrowly focused.

DOI: 10.4324/9781003352853-3

Hegel's mature philosophy is most systematically presented in his 1806 masterpiece, *The Phenomenology of Spirit.* This work examines the historical development of the Western modern Subject and Culture (*Spirit*), which Hegel identifies as the pinnacle of human rationality. For Hegel, the Subject and Spirit are deeply interconnected: the Subject both shapes and is shaped by its cultural context. Hegel's philosophy reflects on their historical evolution, which progresses dialectically – hence his method is often referred to as "historical dialectics".

Hegel's philosophy is deeply rooted in the context of his time, addressing the existential and cultural ruptures that preoccupied his generation. These ruptures – perceived as tragically irreconcilable – arose between the Subject and Nature, Society, or the State, as well as internally, between body and mind. These unresolved tensions led to widespread despair, prompting Hegel to propose a unified concept of Subject/Spirit that could reconcile such divisions. In *The Phenomenology of Spirit*, this reconciliation is presented as a developmental narrative, often likened to a *Bildungsroman* (a coming-of-age story, popularized by Goethe's *Wilhelm Meister*). Here, the protagonist – consciousness – progresses from "natural consciousness" to "Absolute knowledge". This journey involves a confrontation with the "Other," which takes various forms (e.g., the world of nature, desire, the body, woman). Through dialectical processes, consciousness repeatedly acts, fails, and learns from its mistakes. With each misstep, it progresses closer to "Absolute knowledge". At this pinnacle, it comes to recognize the Other as an integral part of its own unified self-identity, hence forming an all-encompassing infinite totality.

In Hegel's philosophy, method and content are inseparable, and negation lies at the core of both. Methodologically, negation is that which drives the dialectical process, with the "law of double negation" resolving contradictions and generating synthesis. Thematically, negation is not merely a logical concept but an active, dynamic force in both thought and reality. In the following sections, I will explore these dimensions. The first section examines Hegel's methodology, while the second and third analyze the role of negation in the world and in thought and language, respectively. The final section investigates the unique nature of the Negative in Hegel's philosophy.

Negation: Driving Force of the Historical Dialectic

The term "dialectic" has deep roots in philosophy, originating with Plato, who introduced it as a method of dialogue in which opposing views (thesis and antithesis) are examined to uncover truth. For Plato, these dialogues could either end in an impasse (*aporia*) or lead to a synthesis of opposites, typically articulated by the philosopher himself (Kojève 1980, 179–180). Hegel transformed this concept, elevating dialectic from a mere method to the very essence of thought, reality, and human history. For Hegel, the dialectic is not just a philosophical tool but a fundamental reflection and description of reality itself (Kojève 1980, 190).

Nonetheless, Hegel employs the dialectic not only as a philosophical principle but also as an *organizing method* for his philosophy as a whole, particularly in *The Phenomenology of Spirit*. The *Phenomenology* unfolds through a series of logically connected dialectical arguments, where each conclusion serves as the starting point for the next. This structure ensures that the philosophical narrative is historically continuous and progressive. Moreover, these dialectical processes are not merely theoretical constructions but are purportedly enacted and experienced by consciousness – the protagonist of the narrative – as it seeks knowledge through encounters with the "Other". At times, Hegel himself, as the omniscient narrator, intervenes to guide the reasoning.

The dialectical process unfolds in three stages, with the second and third stages driven by acts of negation. First, a thesis (a position or idea) is posited – for example, "The cat is black" or "Knowledge is gained through sense perception". Next, *an act of negation* introduces an antithesis that contradicts the thesis: "The cat is not black" or "It is not the case that knowledge is gained through sense perception". This contradiction ("The cat is black and not black") appears irreconcilable. However, in the third stage, *a second act of negation* (the negation of the negation) resolves the contradiction, resulting in a synthesis: "It is not the case that the cat is not black", which, as will be explained, is equivalent to "The cat is black". This synthesis unites the thesis and antithesis into a new identity – not a simple return to the original thesis but a higher-level identity that incorporates and preserves the internal differences. This new unity is more intricate and enriched, shaped by the tension between opposites.

Hegel's conception of this process can be summarized as moving through the following stages: (1) Primary identity (thesis): A = A; (2) Contradiction (thesis and antithesis): A and not-A; (3) Dialectical identity (synthesis): A = not (not-A). To illustrate this structure, replacing "A" with "I" (self) and "not-A" with "not-I" (Other) provides clarity. The primary identity, "I = I", is static and adds nothing new about the self. In contrast, the dialectical identity, "I = I and not (not-I)" or "I = I and not Other", incorporates the Other into the self. This incorporation of internal difference transforms identity into something dynamic, enabling movement and interaction between opposites. This dynamic identity opens up new possibilities. For instance, it allows the self to engage in internal dialogue, such as when one critiques oneself ("You ate too much chocolate"), treating oneself as both "I" and "Other". In this way, the self (consciousness) attains the capacity for self-reflection and self-knowledge – becoming self-conscious. Static identity, by contrast, cannot achieve this level of complexity or self-awareness.

Hegel refers to this latter process, which produces dialectical identity, as *Aufhebung* (often translated as "sublation" or "supersession"), a form of negation that simultaneously *negates and preserves* its object (or content) while *elevating* it to a higher level. Unlike "absolute negation", which annihilates and leaves behind a void, *Aufhebung* is a negation that transforms and enriches the content it acts upon. Through this process, the second negation in the dialectical procedure produces the "dialectical identity", which elevates consciousness to a higher level of knowledge and existence (e.g., enabling it to achieve self-consciousness and introspection).

In Hegel's system (or narrative), the synthesis of one dialectical process immediately becomes the thesis of a new one. This iterative process continues until consciousness reaches "Absolute Knowledge", the point at which all "Others" are *aufgehoben* – negated, preserved, and incorporated into the self. At this ultimate stage, self-consciousness becomes infinite as no "Other" remains external to it to serve as a limitation. Through this narrative of successive dialectical movements, Hegel charts the historical development of (Western) human knowledge and culture, culminating in his Modern era. While individual dialectical moments on the path to "Absolute Knowledge" are necessarily flawed and transient, the system as a whole reaches Truth at its apex.

For Hegel, the advancement of rational thought is driven by its inherently negative nature, which disrupts static identities by introducing contradictions that demand resolution. Negation injects dynamism into consciousness – and into the world – fuelling its movement and development. As Hegel famously writes: "*Contradiction is the root of all movement and life*; it is only in so far as something has a contradiction within it that it moves, is possessed of instinct and activity" (Hegel 2010, 382, emphasis added). This internal tension propels the dialectical process, in which negation-as-supersession resolves contradictions through the "law of double negation".

In *The Phenomenology of Spirit*, Hegel portrays consciousness as undergoing an ongoing journey of self-constitution, one that cycles through conflict and resolution (thesis–antithesis–synthesis) until it ultimately achieves reconciliation in "Absolute Knowledge". At this stage, self-consciousness attains complete unity with itself and the world, fully integrating all previous breaches or contradictions into a cohesive totality.

Negation as Life's Vitality

The previous section outlined the methodological aspect of Hegel's system, but this cannot be separated from its thematic aspect, as negation, for Hegel, is an operation inherent to thought itself. The dialectical process is not an external philosophical tool but the intrinsic mechanism of rationality, driving the historical evolution of human knowledge and culture. Negation, therefore, is fundamental to consciousness's ability to constitute itself as "Absolute Knowledge".

Hegel contends that the human Subject develops through two interconnected activities: thought (which depends on language) and physical work, operating in the theoretical and practical spheres, respectively. Although distinct, these activities are inter-dependent: thought without physical work is powerless to shape the objective world, while work without thought reduces con-sciousness to mere brute, animalistic behavior, leaving the world unchanged. Thought and work together, on the other hand, transform and shape the natural world in alignment with human ideas and goals. This section will focus on negation within the practical sphere – specifically, within the natural world – while the next will examine its role in thought and language.

For Hegel, negation is the vital principle at the core of life itself – its inner driving force. In his philosophy, "Life" refers to the natural world, governed by perpetual forces and laws. Nature is propelled by a "desire" or "lustful emptiness", as organisms strive to fill internal voids. However, the satisfaction of desire is always temporary, inevitably leading to the reemergence of desire. This cycle of fulfilment and renewal is expressed through acts of "consumption", which are, fundamentally, acts of negation. For instance, when a leopard hunts and devours a deer, it "negates" the deer; similarly, when a flower outgrows its bud, it "negates" the bud. Even inanimate processes, such as water eroding rock, embody this principle of negation. All of nature, subject to the passage of time, exists in a state of constant flux – creation and destruction, movement and change – all driven by the negation of an "other". This principle operates on two levels: at the level of particular entities that "negate" one another, and universally, as the natural world as a whole sustains itself by continuously negating and reproducing its particulars. Being, therefore, is an unending pro-cess of *becoming*.

Becoming unfolds in time, and time itself functions as a con-tinuous act of negation: every passing moment is a present that transforms into the past. The "now" is negated and becomes a moment that is no longer – it becomes a moment that *was*. Simi-larly, time negates the particulars that make up the world. When something changes over time, it becomes something *other* than itself; in other words, time negates its present form, so it no longer exists as it once did. However, as Hegel explains through the concept of "determinate negation", this negation does not result in pure nothingness. Instead, it leads to transformation, where the negated entity assumes a new form, becoming something it previously *was not.*

Work, for Hegel, is the means by which embodied, autonomous consciousness engages with and transforms the world. The material world is the "negative" – the "not-I" or "other" of consciousness. It defines what consciousness is not and, simultaneously, what is hostile to it and threatens to negate it. Through labor, however, consciousness "negates the negative" superseding its opposition to the material world. By working on and shaping the material world in accordance with its own ideas, goals, and values, consciousness leaves its unique mark on it. Labor thus becomes an expression of both humanity and individuality, as it externalizes and enriches consciousness's unique personality.

On a social level, work reflects the community's ability to control and shape the material world, enabling it to transcend *natural* laws and replace them with *normative* social rules and values. By transforming the world to align with these norms, the community creates a cultural space – a "home" within the world – where it can live in a distinctly human way. Specifically, the satisfaction of natural needs and desires is suppressed or refined and restructured according to the community's norms. This concept resonates with Freud's later idea of sublimation, introduced nearly a century afterward.

The Negativity of Language

> The word is already a presence made of absence.
>
> (Lacan 2006, 228)

For Hegel, language conditions thought, making the latter impossible without the former. Words (or concepts) acquire determinate meanings that establish the stable, self-same identities of things, which would otherwise remain in constant flux. This process, for Hegel, is mediated by negation.

Hegel illustrates how words gain meaning through the example of the word "now". The challenge in this case is that everything, including speech, is subject to constant change and negation by time. In simplified terms, Hegel's dialectical argument proceeds as follows: Consciousness attempts to signify the present moment by saying "now", but as soon as the word is uttered, the moment has already passed. Thus, what consciousness actually pointed to was a "not-now". To signify the present, consciousness must negate this negation. By doing so, it returns to the assertion that "now is" (Hegel 1977, §107, 63). However, at this point, "now" is understood as a dialectical unity: "now and not (not-now)". It signifies not only the present moment but also other moments (not-nows) that can be identified with the present. In this way, "now" is transformed into *a universal concept*, applicable to moments, days, or even years, depending on the context (Hegel 1977, 63). More broadly, Hegel argues that words are complex, dialectically constituted structures that are general, abstract, and *mediated by negation*. They supersede the fleeting, transient nature of time and thereby become determinate. The same process, Hegel claims, applies to other words, such as "here" and "I", or to object names like "tree" or "house". Words grant objects fixed identities, transcending their fluid and ever-changing nature over time. As Lacan aptly puts it, "concepts, in preserving the duration of what passes away, engender things" (Lacan 2006, 228).

Furthermore, Hegel raises a related point that would profoundly influence future theories of language. When someone says, for example, "tree" and means this particular tree, they refer to something singular, physical, and concrete. However, they determine it using a universal word or concept, which is inherently general and abstract. As a result, the particular tree loses its singular, material nature and becomes the *opposite* of what it is – it is *negated*. In Lacan's terms, the word "kills" the thing. As a universal, the word "tree" applies to any tree or all trees, with the dramatic consequence that the utterance "tree" can never fully signify *this* specific, individual tree. It is, in fact, the nature of language that the singular always remains beyond its reach. This is why Hegel says:

> we do not strictly say what [...] we *mean* to say. But language [...] is the more truthful; in it, we ourselves directly refute what we *mean* to say [...] it is just not possible for us ever to say, or express in words, a sensuous being that we *mean*.
>
> (Hegel 1977, §97, 60, emphasis in original)

This highlights an unbridgeable gap between language and the real, sensuous world, which becomes irretrievably lost in the act of naming. As Hegel explains, "If they actually wanted to *say* 'this' bit of paper which they meant, if they wanted to *say* it, then this is impossible, because the sensuous This that is meant *cannot be reached* by language" (Hegel 1977, §110, 66, emphasis in original). Michal Ben-Naftali further elaborates:

> The word provides me with the thing to which I refer by negating its concrete presence in reality. [...] Language rests on the vanishing of the thing that is replaced by a name. [...] Every utterance [...] originates in a dialectical act of negation in which the negated things are substituted for their meaning.
>
> (Ben-Naftali 2011, 278, my translation)

"Dwelling on the Negative"

Within Hegel's oeuvre, several striking remarks on the Negative stand out, underscoring its profound nature and pivotal role in his dialectical philosophy. In a seminal passage from the Introduction to *The Phenomenology of Spirit*, Hegel writes:

> The activity of division is the force and labour of the *Understanding*, the most astonishing and greatest of powers, or rather the absolute power. The circle that remains self-enclosed and, as substance, holds its moments, is the immediate relationship and therefore arouses no astonishment. But that the accidental as such, detached from its surroundings, that what is bound and is actual only in its connection with other things, attains a Being-there of its own

and a separate freedom – *this is the tremendous power of the negative*; it is the energy of thinking, of the pure I.

(Hegel 1977, §32, 18–19, emphasis added)

Here, Hegel reflects on the role of the Understanding – cognitive thought. He asserts that its power lies in its ability to negate, thereby conceptualizing and introducing division into a stagnant and self-perpetuating unified world. The Understanding wields "tremendous power" because it can divide in thought what cannot be separated in reality. For instance, consider a red ball: in reality, the redness cannot be separated from the ball itself. Yet thought can disconnect them, by conceptualizing and naming the property of redness with one term and the whole object of the ball with another. Neither sensibility nor physical labor can achieve this; it is a unique capacity of the Understanding, which relies on negation to distinguish and determine the meanings of concepts, enabling the dissection of inseparable things (such as the properties of objects distinct from the objects themselves, or a head distinct from the body).

This negative power is inherently destructive, capable of dismantling unified wholes. Yet it is also astonishingly creative, allowing for the production of meaning, language, and knowledge. These, in turn, can be applied to the material world to create new things and, more broadly, contribute to the process of self-development.

Hegel notes that this power is accompanied by deep anxiety:

Death, if that is what we want to call this non-actuality, is the most dreadful thing, and to hold fast what is dead requires the greatest force. [...] But the life of the Spirit is not the life that shrinks from death and keeps clear of devastation; it is the life that endures death and preserves itself in it. Spirit gains its truth only when, in absolute disintegration, it finds itself. It is this power, not as the positive which averts its eyes from the negative, as when we say of something that it is nothing or false, and then, finished with it, turn away and pass on to something else; *Spirit is this power only by looking*

> *the negative in the face, and by dwelling on it. Dwelling on*
> *the negative is the magic force* that converts it into Being.
> (Hegel 1977, §32, 19, emphasis added)

Within his historical account of the subject's self-constitution, Hegel depicts moments where negation is not only directed outward, toward external things, but also inward, toward the subject itself – for example, onto its physical body and natural desires. While it is impossible to recount the entire dialectical process suggested by Hegel here, suffice it to say that consciousness undergoes an extreme act of self-negation, experiencing itself as the utter opposite or *negative* of what it originally was. Consciousness is transformed from an abstract, thinking, knowledge-creating entity into an animal-like, unconscious being driven solely by natural needs and desires. Slavoj Žižek (2007) interprets this moment of self-loss, where consciousness becomes entirely *other* to itself, as an experience of crossing through a "zero point", a "dark abyss" of self-annulment. Rather than fleeing from or rejecting the negative – contradiction, self-otherness, self-negation – Hegel urges us to confront it directly, engaging with it as the driving force behind self-development. Enduring the death-like experience bound to self-negation – *dwelling on the negative* – becomes the transformative force that enables the uniquely human form of life to emerge.

Specifically, this seemingly devastating act of self-destruction is revealed by Hegel to be merely one stage in the process of self-supersession (*Aufhebung*). To truly transcend itself, consciousness must endure and *fully experience* this process. The dialectical progression culminates in the reconstitution of consciousness as an embodied, self-conscious, and autonomous being, independent of natural determination – one that integrates its original self (consciousness) with its otherness or negativity (its physical body) to achieve a higher level of self-knowledge and existence. By incorporating this negativity into its self-identity, consciousness elevates itself to a more capable and sophisticated form of being.

At the core of consciousness's self-identity, Hegel argues, lies negativity or nothingness – self-absence, *un*consciousness, a violent and traumatic nature. Despite its dreadful nature, this negativity is essential for the subject's self-constitution and self-definition – for becoming fully human. Hegel expresses this vividly in *The Philosophy of Spirit*:

> The human being is this Night, this empty nothing which contains everything in its simplicity – a wealth of infinitely many representations, images, none of which occur to it directly, and none of which are not present. This [is] the Night, the interior of [human] nature, existing here – pure Self – [and] in phantasmagoric representations it is night everywhere: here a bloody head suddenly shoots up and there another white shape, only to disappear as suddenly. We see this Night when we look a human being in the eye, looking into a Night which turns terrifying.
>
> (Hegel 1983, Part I. A)

Here, Hegel alludes to an unconscious treasure house (or perhaps a cellar?) where unorganized and unregulated latent images and representations reside – neither fully accessible to consciousness nor entirely absent. This space allows "phantasmagoric representations" to flicker into and out of awareness. While this is not precisely Freud's concept of the unconscious – since repression is absent from Hegel's framework – it can nonetheless be seen as a precursor to it. Furthermore, this "night", this dark abyss of subjectivity – devastating, anxiety-provoking, and transformative – evokes Freud's notion of the destructive or death drives. These drives, as Freud discusses in "Negation", are explicitly linked to disintegration and negation. I now turn to Freud's conception of negation.

Recommended Reading

Kojève, Alexandre. 1980. *Introduction to the Reading of Hegel: Lectures on the Phenomenology of Spirit*. Translated by James H.NicholsJr. Ithaca and London: Cornell University Press.

Pinkard, Terry. 1994. *Hegel's Phenomenology: The Sociality of Reason*. Cambridge: Cambridge University Press.

Taylor, Charles. 1975. *Hegel*. Cambridge: Cambridge University Press.

Reference List

Ben-Naftali, Michal. 2011. *Maurice Blanchot*. Israel: Hakibbutz Hameu-chad Publishing House. [In Hebrew].

Hegel, G. W. F. 1977. *The Phenomenology of Spirit*. Oxford: Oxford University Press.

Hegel, G. W. F. 1983. "Jena Lectures on the Philosophy of Spirit". In *Hegel and the Human Spirit*. Translated by Leo Rauch. Detroit: Wayne State University Press. www.marxists.org/reference/archive/hegel/works/jl/index.htm.

Hegel, G. W. F. 2010. *The Science of Logic*. Translated by George Di Giovanni. Cambridge: Cambridge University Press.

Hyppolite, Jean. 1979. *Genesis and Structure of Hegel's Phenomenology of Spirit*. Translated by Samuel Cherniak and John Heckman. Evanston: Northwestern University Press.

Kojève, Alexandre. 1980. *Introduction to the Reading of Hegel: Lectures on the Phenomenology of Spirit*. Translated by James H.NicholsJr. Ithaca and London: Cornell University Press.

Lacan, Jacques. 2006. *Écrits: The First Complete Edition in English*. Translated by Bruce Fink. London and New York: W. W. Norton & Company.

Rockmore, Tom. 2010. *Kant and Phenomenology*. Chicago: University of Chicago Press. doi:10.7208/9780226723419.

Žižek, Slavoj. 2007. *Enjoy Your Symptom!: Jacques Lacan in Hollywood and Out*. London and New York: Routledge.

Chapter 3

Freud on Negation

The concept of negation is present in Freud's thought from the beginning, appearing in various forms. As Green points out, negation is already evident in Freud's key concept – the *un*conscious. In this chapter, I will address three issues. First, I will examine Freud's intriguing claim that the unconscious lacks the symbol of "no" by exploring its negation-less logic and how this shapes the contents of the unconscious. Second, I will outline a "developmental narrative" of the various unconscious negative mechanisms that, according to Freud, lead to the establishment of symbolic negation. This will involve examining a selection of Freud's writings in chronological order to reveal what makes certain mechanisms "negative" in his thought and to trace his perception of how negation develops within the psyche. Finally, I will provide a close reading of Freud's seminal essay "Negation" (1925), which further illuminates the unconscious and conscious meanings of negation in Freud's work and connects the various issues discussed in this chapter.

The Negation-less Logic of the Unconscious

In his inaugural book, *The Interpretation of Dreams* (1900), Freud notes several unique and interrelated characteristics of dreams:

> The attitude of dreams to the category of antithesis and contradiction is very striking. This category is simply

DOI: 10.4324/9781003352853-4

ignored; the word No does not seem to exist for a dream. Dreams are particularly fond of reducing antitheses to uniformity or representing them as one and the same thing. Dreams likewise take the liberty of representing any element whatever by its desired opposite, so that it is at first impossible to tell, in respect of any element which is capable of having an opposite, whether it is contained in the dream-thoughts in the negative or the positive sense.

(Freud 1900, 516–517)

Forty years later, in *An Outline of Psycho-Analysis* (1940), Freud revisits and expands on these same ideas, now referring to the unconscious (Ucs.) in general and using the terminology of the second topic:

The governing rules of logic carry no weight in the unconscious; it might be called the Realm of the Illogical. Urges with contrary aims exist side by side in the unconscious without any need arising for an adjustment between them. Either they have no influence whatever on each other, or, if they have, no decision is reached, but a compromise comes about which is nonsensical since it embraces mutually incompatible details. With this is connected the fact that contraries are not kept apart but treated as though they were identical, so that in the manifest dream any element may also have the meaning of its opposite.

(Freud 1940, 4979)

We have found that processes in the unconscious or in the id obey different laws from those in the preconscious ego. We name these laws in their totality the primary process, in contrast to the secondary process which governs the course of events in the preconscious, in the ego.

(Freud 1940, 4974)

Freud claims that the dream does not contain the symbol of negation and that the contradictions within it – those connecting irreconcilable claims – "pass" without regard to their problematic nature. In logical terms, this means that while contradictions exist in dreams, the law of non-contradiction does not apply. Rather than becoming rivals that negate or neutralize each other, opposing contents coexist within a dream in unity or replace each other with indifference. As the second and third quotes make clear, Freud asserts that the unconscious (Ucs.) is not logical – or, alternatively, that it operates according to different logical principles.

But what does logic without negation look like, and how does it function? How can the absence of negation in the unconscious be explained? Does this claim truly imply that unconscious contents cannot be formulated in the negative or cannot be false? To address these questions, it is useful to examine additional characteristics of dream life that Freud outlines in *The Interpretation of Dreams*. First, Freud argues that, unlike the waking state, in which mental activity is ideational – carried out in the form of ideas and representations "by means of verbal images and language" (1900, 119) – dreams rely on mental activity in the form of images (both visual and auditory). In other words, "the dream hallucinates – that is, […] it replaces thoughts by hallucinations" (117).

Second, the quality and sense of reality in dream images are similar to those of sensory perception rather than memory. Thus, a dream "represent[s] something *as actually present*" (118, italics added). In other words, the events in a dream are experienced as if they had occurred objectively – with the same vividness and believability as events in real life. Third, a part of this effect stems from the way dream images are combined to create a scene or "situation": they "dramatize an idea" (118). This dramatization leads to the belief that the events in a dream are truly experienced and not merely intellectual ("only in one's head"). It is only upon waking that one realizes they have merely dreamed. With no criterion to distinguish between sensory experiences originating from within and those arriving (during the waking state) from without, "the dream-elements are […] *true and actual experiences of the psyche*, similar to those which come to the waking state by way of the senses" (119, italics added).

Freud's claim that dreams are realized in the form of images, rather than linguistic representations, explains why the sign "no" does not exist in dreams. If "no" does not exist in dreams, then contents cannot be formulated in negative terms, nor can they be false. The entire category of claims like "X is not…" or "It is not the case that…" is impossible in dreams.

To clarify and justify these claims, I suggest looking at René Magritte's painting *The Treachery of Images.* In this work, a pipe is beautifully painted, and beneath it is the statement "This is not a pipe". What is the relationship between these two elements – the image and the statement? The statement denies that the image is what it appears to be, but the image itself remains undeniable, mocking the statement by refusing to yield to it. In fact, the negative statement disavowing the image of the pipe remains powerless. This occurs because, as a rule, *images resist denial* – that is, they resist negation through words. The painting reveals a profound insight: once we see an image, language cannot erase it from our consciousness.

Furthermore, if Magritte had wanted to paint a "denied" or "negative" pipe, what would the picture look like? How could one visually represent an image equivalent to the statement "This is not a pipe", "It is not the case that this is a pipe", or, rather, "This pipe does not exist"? Marking an X on the picture, for instance, as a symbolic gesture of negation, would merely present a visual version of the "paradox of negative judgment", which, as discussed in the first chapter, haunts negative claims that aim to deny the existence of something. The paradox arises because, in order to deny the existence of something (e.g., "this pipe does not exist"), one must first conceptually or linguistically refer to that "something" as if it exists, at least in thought. This act of reference creates a logical tension: How can one negate the existence of something that must first be acknowledged in order to deny it? In the present case, the image whose existence ("this pipe does not exist") or identity ("this is not a pipe") is denied must first be represented "positively". However, its symbolic negation would not suffice: if the picture remains visible, the negation will fail; yet if it is completely covered, it will become impossible to know *what* has been negated. Thus, the paradox persists.

The image, I suggest, has the status and power of *a fact in the world*, and this is equally applicable to the realm of dreams. Unconscious dream contents can be regarded as having the ontological status of *facts*. Like facts, they form a primary and fundamental stratum that is ineffable in itself – its meaning being something we must confer – but provides the raw material for epistemological or hermeneutic inquiry. These contents lend themselves to translation and, consequently, to (clinical) interpretation or (metapsychological) theorization. Moreover, such contents present themselves only in positive terms – that is, they show what there *is*, not what there is *not* – and possess only one truth value, meaning they cannot be false. They cannot be false because, like sensory perceptions, they are experienced directly and immediately as present realities within the dream. They do not make propositional claims or assert truths that could be judged as true or false; instead, they simply *are* – they show what exists in the dream world. Since there is no negation or contradiction within the dream's logic, the concept of falsehood does not apply to its contents. Finally, phenomenologically, and in agreement with Freud's observations, dream contents – much like sense perceptions of external facts – are experienced as actually and truly *present*.

This suggestion aligns with – and can be interpreted as a way of understanding – Freud's comparison between the difference of dream thought and dream content in two distinct languages:

> The dream-thoughts and the dream-content are presented to us like two versions of the same subject-matter in two different languages. Or, more properly, the dream-content seems like a transcript of the dream-thoughts *into another mode of expression*, whose characters and syntactic laws it is our business to discover by comparing the original and the translation. The dream-thoughts are immediately comprehensible, as soon as we have learnt them. The dream-content, on the other hand, is expressed as it were in a pictographic script, the characters of which have to be transposed individually into the language of the dream-thoughts.
>
> (Freud SE 4, 277, in Rayner and Tuckett 1988, 4)

In light of these understandings, an intriguing question arises: How can a contradiction be expressed in a dream or in the unconscious in general, without the possibility of negation? After all, a contradiction consists of two opposing statements (or contents), with one negating what the other affirms. To explore this question, Freud's analysis of a dream, presented immediately after the quote at the beginning of this chapter, provides a useful starting point.

Freud describes a case in which a woman dreamed she was holding a flowering bough in her hands. He argues that the bough condensed into a single symbol both her satisfaction at having been able to protect her sexual purity and her sense of guilt over her promiscuous behavior. He writes:

> The same blossoming bough [...] represents at once sexual innocence and its opposite. Moreover, the same dream, which expresses the dreamer's joy at having succeeded in passing through life unsullied, hints in several places (as in the falling of the blossom) at the opposite train of thought, namely, that she had been guilty of various sins against sexual purity (that is, in her childhood). In the analysis of the dream we may clearly distinguish the two trains of thought, of which the comforting one seems to be superficial, and the reproachful one more profound. *The two are diametrically opposed to each other, and their similar yet contrasting elements have been represented by identical dream-elements.*
>
> (Freud 1900, 679–680, italics added)

The blooming branch in the dream symbolizes opposing elements: a lily stem and a camellia, representing purity and promiscuity, respectively, thereby expressing two opposing "trains of thought". These contrasts are created without the use of negation, instead being represented through two "positive images" with opposing cultural connotations of femininity. Through the image of the lily stem, symbolizing purity, the dreamer's belief "I am not promiscuous" is positively represented, while through the camellia, which implies menstruation and impure behavior, the claim "I am not pure" is reframed positively as "I am promiscuous". This mechanism introduces antithesis into the dream without relying on negative formulations.

Furthermore, the dream conveys preference or judgment without negation by assigning greater weight to one of the opposing options. It achieves this by making the "comforting" belief appear "superficial" and the "reproachful" belief more "profound" (Freud 1900, 681; Saad 2020, 249). This subtle weighting demonstrates which option the dreamer views as more significant or "correct" without needing to negate the other, avoiding the explicit formulation of "it is not the case that."

Another logical operation present in classical logic but absent in the negation-free logic of the unconscious (Ucs.) is "either… or" (exclusive disjunction). As Amit Saad explains, this form of logical relation is governed in classical logic by the "law of the excluded middle", which states that every claim must be either true or false, ruling out the possibility of a third (middle) option. In this framework, each alternative necessarily excludes the other (e.g., "Michael either likes broccoli or does not like broccoli"). However, in the logic of the dream, since it is impossible to determine that a claim is false, all claims must be true (Saad 2020, 245). Consequently, the principle of exclusive disjunction is absent from the dream's logic.

Freud himself is aware of this and offers guidance on how the analyst should interpret this phenomenon:

> The alternative "either-or" cannot be expressed in dreams in any way whatever. Both of the alternatives are usually inserted in the text of the dreams as though they were equally valid. […] If, however, in reproducing a dream, its narrator feels inclined to make use of an "either-or" – e.g. "it was either a garden or a sitting-room" – what was present in the dream-thoughts was not an alternative but an "and", a simple addition.
>
> (Freud 1900, 316–7, cited in Saad 2020, 248)

The replacement of "or" with "and" reflects the general tendency of the dream or Ucs. towards unity. Rayner and Tuckett, after reviewing a comprehensive list of Freudian features of the Ucs., reached the following conclusion:

> One trait does, however, appear to be common to all thirteen characteristics; this is that they unite or unify things which for ordinary thinking are distinct and separated. The absence of contradiction unites things which are quite distinct in ordinary thinking – when something is affirmed and something is denied.
>
> (Rayner and Tuckett 1988, 16)

The absence of the law of non-contradiction and the law of the excluded middle, which logically follows from the non-existence of symbolic negation, underpins this tendency towards *unity*. While the dream contains various different elements, these elements are added together, placed side by side, or united into condensed objects or people, rather than being separated or excluded from one another (as illustrated by Freud's patient's dream above). Freud states that "[t]he mechanism of dream-formation is favourable in the highest degree to only one of the logical relations. This relation is that of *similarity, agreement, contiguity, just as*" (Freud 1900, 681, italics added).

In contrast, the dream avoids the alternative logical relation of difference, disagreement, separation, or variation – relations that are characteristic of conscious thought (or, in Hegelian terms, the Understanding). This overarching tendency towards unity aligns with the absence of negation, since, as previously discussed, negation is precisely what disrupts or destroys unity.

The Evolution of Negation: A Chronological Outline

This section examines how Freud conceptualizes key "negative" mechanisms throughout his evolving psychoanalytic theorization. Freud consistently mentions these mechanisms together while organizing them in a hierarchical order of evolution and sophistication, enabling us to identify which mechanisms he considers negative. By reflecting on these mechanisms, I aim to answer two questions: What makes certain psychic mechanisms negative, according to Freud? And how does Freud conceive of the mental evolution of negation – both developmentally and in terms of complexity?

In *The Interpretation of Dreams*, Freud identifies negation as a linguistic sign and a function of thought. However, as he explains in the 1895 "Project for a Scientific Psychology" (in neurophysiological terms), the initial processes in the Ucs. system precede thought. This does not mean Freud assumes the Ucs. lacks negative *mental mechanisms*. On the contrary, he refers to various unconscious, pre-linguistic actions as forms of negation. Though possessing operative value, these forms of negation are presented as precursors to linguistic negation, preparing the ground for its development. In this sense, they can be identified as *proto-negation*. I will now examine these forms and their evolutionary progression, following Freud's thought as expressed in a selection of texts chronologically.

In the "Project", Freud distinguishes two systems or functions in the Ucs. The "primary neuronic system" is constitutional, maintaining the somatopsychic apparatus in balance (homeostasis) by discharging energy generated by external and internal stimuli, in line with what Freud later calls the "pleasure principle". However, Freud argues that while the primary system effectively handles external stimuli – through flight – it is less effective against endogenous stimuli originating from the body. These stimuli produce primary needs like hunger, breathing, and sexuality, which cannot be avoided. Moreover, tension reduction for some of these stimuli requires a "specific action" by an external object, such as feeding by the caregiver. For this external action to occur, the immediate hallucinatory relief achieved by cathecting the memory of the object (formed after perceiving the external object) must be resisted. Resistance is necessary because this course of action, while initiating satisfaction, does not produce real biological satisfaction. Thus, discharge must be postponed until a real object perception takes place.

This procedure requires a criterion to distinguish between the idea or hallucination of an object and the real perception of that object. Such a criterion – referred to by Freud as the "indication of quality or reality" – emerges with the development of the secondary system. This system, comprising both thought and the consolidation of the ego, allows *inhibition* to occur. As Freud explains, "[i]nhibition on the part of the ego leads to a moderation of the cathexis of the object wished-for, which makes it possible for that object to be recognized as not being a real one" (1895, 389). According to Freud, thought and judgment arise from "[t]he difference between the idea and the perception" (418), which is identified through the evolving capacity for reality testing. Inhibition of the primary system (reflex) creates a deferral of discharge, freeing thought from the exclusive regulation of the pleasure principle and enabling *judgment*.

Interestingly, in line with the philosophical terms used earlier chapters, Freud emphasizes that achieving real satisfaction results in a state of identity, which is "the aim and end of all processes of thought". He further explains, "[c]ognitive or judging thought seeks identity with somatic cathexis; reproductive thought seeks for an identity with psychical cathexis (an experience of the subject's own)" (394). However, for this identity with a real object to be achieved, the ego must first negate the "false" identity offered by hallucination. Thus, inhibition functions as a primitive proto-negation mechanism, representing a level of sophistication above somatopsychic defenses, such as reflexes like flight from pain or oral expulsion.

In the same text, Freud examines another significant form of negative mental mechanism: *repression* (*Verdrängung*). His treatment of this concept is preliminary and tentative, presented hesitantly, differing from the confident tone of the rest of the book, and his position is modified towards its end. Strachey notes that Freud never completed the fourth part of the book, originally planned to address repression in depth, due to doubts about his ideas at the time (349). Repression, a cornerstone of psychoanalysis, is a major form of proto-negation. Initially, Freud equated repression with defense, though he later classified it as one (albeit prominent) defense mechanism among others. Within Freud's theory of proto-negation mechanisms, which precondition the development of symbolic negation, repression plays a central role. Its meaning evolved throughout Freud's writings. In the following paragraphs, I will briefly outline his thinking on repression as it relates to other negative mental mechanisms.

At the beginning of Freud's "Project", repression is described as a primary defense mechanism in which cathexis is quickly withdrawn from a distressing memory-image following a painful experience (383). In this sense, repression responds to "internal pain" in the same way that flight responds to external painful stimuli. Later in the text, Freud distinguishes repression from primary defense and redefines it as a defensive process applied "exclusively [...] to ideas that, firstly, arouse a distressing affect (unpleasure) in the ego, and that, secondly, relate to sexual life" (408). However, when analyzing clinical cases of hysteria and obsessional neurosis, Freud becomes puzzled by the inconsistencies in the conditions under which repression occurs. He is particularly confounded by why repression is consistently tied to unpleasant sexual affects, while other, non-sexual but equally distressing affects do not trigger this mechanism. Freud concludes that "the process of repression remains the core of the riddle" (410).

During this period of Freud's work, marked by publications such as *Studies on Hysteria* (1895) and "Further Remarks on the Defence Neuro-Psychoses" (1896), repression is identified primarily as a pathological mental mechanism linked to childhood sexual trauma and neuropsychoses. At this stage, Freud treats repression and defense as synonymous, describing repression as "the psychic mechanism of (unconscious) defense" (1896) (Bren-Brenner 1957, 21).

In *The Interpretation of Dreams* (1900), Freud expands on repression, introducing foundational concepts like the distinction between primary and secondary mental processes in the Ucs. and Pcs. systems, cathexis, and the pleasure principle (frequently referred to here as the "pain principle") (Brenner 1957, 26). In chapter VII, Freud refines the concept of repression by distinguishing between "primary repression" and "repression proper". Primary repression is an unconscious mechanism present from the beginning of life that represses infantile wishes and memories in line with the pleasure principle. These repressed experiences, irretrievable for the Pcs., form the core and "the precondition of all later instances of repression" (Brenner 1957, 27).

"Repression proper", in contrast, acts on preconscious derivatives of these infantile experiences, decathecting and expelling them into the Ucs. This form of repression encounters resistance when, due to organic changes (e.g., puberty), these derivatives push upward toward consciousness. As Brenner explains, "the Pcs. would intensify its way of opposing the repressed ideas, i.e., its counter-cathexes, which it had previously erected, but eventually the repressed ideas would force their way through to consciousness" in the form of symptoms, or alternatively through dreams, jokes, or slips of a tongue (27).

This understanding demonstrates why repression is a form of proto-negation: it blocks the natural tendency of impulses and ideas to discharge or rise to consciousness by exerting a *counter-force* (31). In this work, Freud revises his earlier view by asserting that repression occurs not only in neurotics but also as part of normal mental development (30). However, he continues to argue that only sexual impulses provoke neurotic symptoms (30).

Freud revisits the concept of repression in *Jokes and Their Relation to the Unconscious* (1905), where he continues to describe repression as the mental apparatus's way of rejecting unpleasant ideas. In developmental terms, he writes: "Repression may, without doubt, be correctly described as the intermediate stage between a defensive reflex and a condemning judgment" (Freud 1905, 126). Here, Freud identifies three negative mental functions – *defensive reflex, repression*, and *judgment* – arranged in ascending developmental sophistication.

In "Formulations on the Two Principles of Mental Functioning" (1911), Freud explains how the reality principle develops and supersedes the pleasure principle, expanding on ideas from his *Project*. He argues that the reality principle emerges from frustration, specifically the failure to achieve satisfaction of internal needs through hallucinatory investment in the object. This failure forces the psyche to abandon hallucination and develop reality testing, which prioritizes reality over pleasure. Reality testing, a process of thinking, equips the psyche to endure arousal tension and postpone discharge. This allows for an "impartial passing of judgment" (Freud 1911, 221), in which ideas are evaluated as true or false based on their consistency with the external world. Freud emphasizes that judgment replaces the pleasurable with the useful (223). This secondary process introduces the determination of truth value, which is absent in the Ucs. *Judgment thus replaces repression*, which had earlier blocked the cathexis of ideas producing displeasure: "[W]hat was presented in the mind was no longer what is agreeable but what was *real*, even if it happened to be disagreeable" (219, italics added). With the advent of thinking and judgment, action becomes possible, replacing or restraining involuntary motor discharge.

However, repression remains dominant in one domain: fantasy. Here, repression continues to act because fantasy is tied closely to sexual instincts, which evade reality testing. Freud argues that while ego instincts grow under the reality principle due to external frustrations, sexual instincts follow a different trajectory. They can achieve satisfaction independently through autoeroticism, avoiding the frustrations that force ego instincts to adapt to reality. As a result, the sexual instincts remain governed by the pleasure principle, and repression continues to inhibit the cathexis of ideas associated with non-pleasure, preventing them from reaching consciousness.

In his 1915 essay "Repression", Freud further refines the concept, defining it as a psychic "resistance" that disables instinctual impulses in consciousness by severing their representatives or associated ideas to avoid displeasure: *"[T]he essence of repression lies simply in turning something away, and keeping it at a distance, from the conscious"* (1915a, 2978, italics in original). By this point, as Brenner notes, Freud no longer views "defense" and "repression" as synonymous but treats repression as one of several mental operations that fall under the broader category of defense (Brenner 1957, 36).

In this text, Freud revisits the developmental explanation he provided in earlier works, offering a narrative for the evolution of proto-negative mechanisms. He begins by emphasizing that repression is not an innate mechanism but a developmental achievement that arises only after a rupture between the Cs. and Ucs. has been established. Prior to this stage, Freud explains, the task of fending off instinctual impulses is managed by other instinctual vicissitudes, such as reversal into the opposite or turning upon the self (1915a, 2978).

Freud also explicitly distinguishes between "primal repression" and "repression proper". Primal repression prevents the ideational representative of the instinct from entering consciousness, whereas repression proper targets ideas stemming from or related to the repressed instinct, even if they arise elsewhere. Freud notes that at a later stage, judgment (condemnation) becomes a favored method for managing instinctual impulses: "*Repression is a preliminary stage of condemnation, something between flight and condemnation*" (Freud 1915a, 2977, italics added).

In "The Unconscious" (1915b), Freud reaffirms the absence of negation in the Ucs., as noted in *The Interpretation of Dreams*, and situates negation within his developmental framework of protoforms: "There are in this system [Ucs.] no negation, no doubt, no degrees of certainty: all this is only introduced by the work of the censorship between the Ucs. and the Pcs. *Negation is a substitute, at a higher level, for repression*" (Freud 1915b, 186, italics added).

In "A Child is Being Beaten" (1919), Freud clarifies that repression does not result from a conflict between derivatives of two different instincts but rather from "a conflict between an acceptable drive derivative on the one hand, and the psychic representative of the outer world on the other" (Brenner 1957, 37).

By the time of "The Problem of Anxiety" (1926), Freud redefines repression in light of his second, structural theory. First, the ego, rather than the Pcs. and Ucs., becomes the repressing agency, with the ego now understood as partly conscious and partly unconscious (Brenner 1957, 38). Second, the conflict between instinctual derivatives and external demands is reframed as a conflict between the id and the ego/superego. Third, Freud broadens the concept of "defense" to include multiple mechanisms employed by the ego to regulate instincts, some of which predate the possibility of repression. Consequently, repression is reserved as a specific type of defense mechanism.

Freud continues to view infantile repression as the foundation for later repression (Brenner 1957, 44). He defines repression as "a mechanism which the ego may employ against an instinctual drive which is the source of anxiety" (43), typically directed at libidinal drives but, in some cases, also at aggressive or destructive drives (Freud 1930). Additionally, repression may target the demands of the superego (Brenner 1957, 43).

The ego employs repression through *countercathexis*, which blocks the drive's entry into consciousness, prevents the emergence of associated affects, and inhibits physical actions aimed at satisfying the drive (44). Brenner notes that repression can also manage instinctual demands and external stimuli through other means, such as judgmental repudiation (44).

This brings us back to the broader narrative of Freud's proto-negative mechanisms, tracing their development and hierarchical organization as outlined throughout his writings. Repression, as an advanced form of proto-negation, represents a key step in the evolution of mental mechanisms, bridging earlier, reflexive defenses and higher-order processes like judgment and reality testing.

As discussed, Freud first situates the formation of negation within the establishment of censorship, a concept belonging to the first topography (later incorporated into the superego in the second topography). Censorship operates at the boundary between the Ucs. and the Pcs.-Cs. systems (Laplanche and Pontalis 1988, 66), deciding which contents may or may not pass from the former to the latter, in line with the reality principle. Derived from the Latin *censere* (to consider), censorship suppresses or prohibits unwanted contents, effectively functioning as a form of judgment involving negation. Thus, *negation becomes "a substitute, at a higher level, for repression"* (Freud 1915a, 186, italics added). As Laplanche and Pontalis explain, the "antagonism" between the Ucs. and Pcs.-Cs. systems, separated by censorship, "corresponds […] to the dualism of the pleasure and reality principles, with the latter seeking to establish its superiority over the former" (Laplanche and Pontalis 1988, 360).

Censorship not only prevents unpleasant contents from entering consciousness by restricting them to the Ucs., but also acts as a two-way permeable barrier. This barrier allows upward movement of repressed material provided it is linguistically negated, or denied. Through this mechanism, the ego can *safely* recognize repressed content – by negating it – without fully accepting it.

While Freud's views on the psychic apparatus evolved over time, his understanding of the developmental trajectory from proto-negation to negation "proper" remained consistent. In Freud's early neurological framework, negative processes such as reflexive flight, rejection, and expulsion were instinctive defense mechanisms. Later defense mechanisms, such as inhibition and repression, became possible with the structural distinctions between Ucs. and Pcs.-Cs. systems in the first topography, or the development of unconscious ego functions capable of opposing id drives in the second topography. These mechanisms primarily protect the psyche or ego from instinctual contents that provoke displeasure or anxiety. Repression, for example, serves a dual function: first, to ensure the real satisfaction of vital biological needs by decathecting fantasies and wishes; and second, to block potentially harmful instincts whose satisfaction in relation to the external world could result in real harm.

In parallel with repression, reality testing emerges, enabling the psyche to evaluate options and reject ineffective, forbidden, or anxiety-provoking alternatives. This process prioritizes the reality principle over the pleasure principle by introducing negation ("no") into the mental apparatus. Negation facilitates judgment, symbol formation, and logical thinking in accordance with the rules of classical logic. Freud's article "Negation" explores the instinctive roots of negation and its developmental stages, particularly as forms of judgment, which will be addressed in the third part of this chapter.

Before that, I would like to conclude this section by identifying the common characteristics of these mental mechanisms and answering the question: What makes them forms of negation? As we have seen, these mechanisms include: *Inhibition of discharge*: countering the natural tendency of instincts to seek immediate gratification and tension relief; *Decathexis*: opposing the libido's investment in fantasies that provide unreal satisfaction; *Repression*: pushing unpleasant contents into the unconscious and resisting the natural tendency of unconscious material to rise to consciousness; *Negation*: maintaining repression while allowing repressed content to enter consciousness in a limited form, avoiding full exposure to its affective meaning.

What unites these mechanisms is their reversal of natural tendencies: they create a *countermovement* by applying a *counterforce* to instinctual drives. Thus, the negativity of psychological mechanisms is revealed, as concluded in the philosophical discussions earlier, to reside in their *directional* action – *opposing and reversing* the natural flow of mental processes.

"Negation" (1925)

The central leitmotif of Freud's 1925 article, as Jean Hyppolite (1966) observes, is that *negation is the birthplace of the intellect.* Freud, however, develops this idea in a layered and convoluted manner. Despite its brevity, the article is dense with ideas and perspectives, and its structure may seem puzzling at first. A closer reading, however, reveals its underlying logic. Freud begins by examining the clinical role of linguistic negation, then traces its roots to primary instinctual processes, expands to a metapsychological and mythological perspective on negation's dual nature, and finally returns to his clinical observations about the unconscious. The argument thus forms a full odyssean circle, enriched by its exploration at various levels.

Freud starts with a clinical observation: the way patients use negation allows unconscious content to surface into consciousness. In his well-known example, a patient discussing a dream says, "You ask who this person in the dream could be. It is not my mother" (Freud 1925, 235). Freud advises analysts to disregard the negative formulation and interpret the content as true. In this case, Freud asserts, the person in the dream *is* the mother. The content must be affirmed not in spite of its denial, but precisely because of it. The denial itself reveals the truth, as the word "no" signals that the statement originates in the unconscious. Negation, Freud claims, creates a pathway for thinking to break free from the Ucs.; it facilitates the liberation of thinking from the constraints of repression. In this way, unconscious content can be expressed by the patient, provided that it is formulated in a negative form. Through negation, the patient simultaneously acknowledges and rejects inconvenient truths.

Freud further emphasizes that by the act of negation "the intellectual function is separated from the affective process" (236). Negation *splits* the repressed content into two parts: the intellectual and the emotional. As an intellectual act, negation can only affect the intellectual aspect of the repressed material, leaving the emotional component untouched and still repressed. This division allows limited intellectual acceptance of the repressed content while preserving the core of the repression. Freud notes that the emotional aspect can only be addressed through prolonged analysis via transference, though, even then, "the repressive process itself" persists (236).

Jean Hyppolite explains this dynamic as the birth of "pure" thought – an intellectual process – out of the original unity of intellectual and emotional elements. Stéphane Mosès translates Freud's argument into logical terms aligned with Hegelian dialectics. Mosès argues that negation is inherently "the negation of repression" (2010, 303). Since repression is itself a form of negation, the patient's denial ("no") cancels the repression – negation negates negation – leading to the affirmation of the repressed content. In this process, negation negates or denies a certain unconscious content while simultaneously preserving it, thus contributing to the patient's self-knowledge. This dynamic reflects the Hegelian concept of *Aufhebung* (supersession), where something is simultaneously canceled, preserved, and elevated to a higher level of complexity and sophistication. Freud explicitly uses the term *Aufhebung* in this context: "Die Verneinung ist eine Art, das Verdrängte zur Kenntnis zu nehmen, eigentlich schon eine Aufhebung der Verdrängung, aber freilich keine Annahme des Verdrängten" (Freud 1925, 236). In translation: "Negation is a way of taking cognizance of the repressed, actually already a lifting (*Aufhebung*) of the repression, though, to be sure, not an acceptance of the repressed." This statement encapsulates the dual function of negation: it brings the repressed into consciousness while maintaining the essence of the repression intact, allowing intellectual engagement without full emotional confrontation.

Following this, Freud turns to a developmental exploration of the "psychological origin" of negation. He begins by reminding us that negation and affirmation are tasks of judgment and argues that to negate something inherently means to want to repress it. Repression, Freud explains, precedes linguistic negation (denial) and is eventually replaced by it. But what is the origin of both repression and negation? Freud locates their roots in oral instincts and identifies two related forms of judgment: the judgment of attribution and the judgment of existence. Let us examine each in turn.

The *judgment of attribution* is rooted in the child's omnipotent world governed by the pleasure principle. It evaluates whether an object (or part of it) is considered good or bad for the child and, accordingly, whether it should be incorporated (swallowed) or expelled (spitted out). The decision that something is bad and must be rejected constitutes *the first negative judgment*: "[E]xpulsion is the origin of negation. This means that the object is undesirable. Therefore, it has to be outside me" (Freud 1925, 313). Mosès adds that this type of judgment is responsible for distinguishing between inside and outside, and specifically, for creating the *extrapsychic* – thereby establishing the object as external. This process, hence, *implicitly* creates the distinction between subject and object, or "I" and "other".

Freud's following statement is particularly insightful: "What is bad, what is alien to the ego and what is external are, to begin with, identical" (1925, 237). The connection Freud suggests here between the notions of what is estranged or other to the ego, what is bad and therefore unwanted, and what is external resonates with his earlier claim in "Instincts and Their Vicissitudes" that "Hate, as a relation to objects, is older than love. It derives from the primal repudiation by the narcissistic ego of the external world with its sources of stimuli" (1915c, 138). Freud explains that hate arises as a response to objects perceived as external and threatening, or as sources of displeasure. In this framework, the differentiation of the object as something external and separate from the ego occurs through acts of rejection or hostility. Thus, the act of repudiation plays a fundamental role in the creation or recognition of the object as distinct from the self. This profoundly suggests that the object is originally constituted out of hostility – or hatred. In terms of our present discussion, this suggests that not only thinking but also the very concept of the *other* is constituted through negation.

At this stage, Mosès raises a puzzlement. Negation, he argues, emerges against a backdrop of absolute affirmation within the pleasure-ego, which is dominated by eros or the libido. The pleasure-ego says "yes" to everything, affirming and introjecting desirable objects: "Affirmation in this domain means introjection of the object. That is to say that the object is desirable" (Mosès 2010, 313). If this is the case, how can negation or expulsion occur within the pleasure-ego? Where does negation originate? Freud provides an answer: "The original pleasure-ego wants to introject everything that is good and to eject from itself everything that is bad" (Freud 1925, 237). On the surface, this explanation seems consistent – negation arises as the pleasure-ego eliminates bad experiences to maintain pleasurable ones. However, as Mosès points out, this claim remains philosophically puzzling, as Freud does not fully address how negation emerges within a framework defined by affirmation. Mosès concludes that this presents "an extremely important philosophical problem that Freud does not thematise" (Mosès 2010, 314–315). Freud does, however, hint at a resolution toward the end of his article, which will be addressed later.

The *judgment of existence*, by contrast, is carried out by the reality-ego, which replaces the pleasure-ego and operates under the reality principle. This type of judgment concerns whether an object, already represented internally, exists only in the infant's mind or also externally in the real world. In other words, it evaluates the ontological status of the object: Does it exist in reality or only hallucinatorily? Freud writes: "What is unreal, merely a presentation and subjective, is only internal; what is real is also there *outside*" (Freud 1925, 237, italics in original).

While this judgment also addresses the distinction between inside and outside, it introduces the subjective-objective distinction. Crucially, Freud emphasizes that the question is not whether an external object corresponding to the internal representation can be *found*, but whether the represented object can be *re-found* in the external world. This distinction arises because representations are formed based on past perceptions of real objects available to the senses. The existence of an external object that initially generated the representation is, therefore, indisputable. The question, instead, is whether the object *still* exists and can be *re*discovered. Freud then adds that "object shall have been lost which once brought real satisfaction" (Freud 1925, 238). In this brief, almost fleeting statement, Freud touches on the essence of human tragedy: the ever-changing and uncertain nature of reality, where things appear and disappear beyond our control – present one moment and gone the next. He highlights the irretrievability of initial bliss provided by the primary object and the reality that any satisfying object will, from then on, be merely an incomplete substitute.

Thinking about the Negative, it is worth noting that the judgment of existence is fundamentally tied to the *absence* of the object. Specifically, the mother or caregiver, due to the necessities of life, cannot always be present with the child but is intermittently absent. This absence prompts the child to search for the object whose representation exists within him or her – outside of herself – and, in doing so, to recognize its independent existence. This means that if the mother were always present, mental growth would not be triggered and, in fact, would become impossible. The absence of the mother introduces the child to the reality of separation and independence, prompting the development of processes such as symbolization, reality testing, object recognition, and the distinction between self and other – all of which are essential for developing a healthy – not psychotic – mental life. As will be demonstrated in the following chapters, the absence of the primary object becomes a central axis around which much of the drama of mental life in general – and the negative in particular – revolves.

Following his analysis of judgment, which connects intellectual negation to the "primary instinctive drives" (Freud 1925, 239), Freud highlights a shared characteristic between judgment (deciding "yes" or "no") and the primary drives (deciding inclusion or exclusion based on the pleasure principle): *polarity*. He argues that the polarity between affirmation and negation corresponds to the duality of the drives: "[a]ffirmation – as a substitute of uniting – belongs to the Eros; negation – the successor to expulsion – belongs to the instinct of destruction" (239). Thus, Freud posits that while the pleasure principle is fueled by the libidinal energy of the life drives, which affirm and introject objects (or parts of them), it is equally influenced by the destructive drives, which result in expulsion – a primitive form of negation that later evolves into the symbolic "no".

Jean Hyppolite, in his close reading of Freud's text (delivered in one of Jacques Lacan's famous seminars), draws attention to Freud's intriguing choice of words: affirmation is described as a *substitute* for union, while negation is framed as a *successor* to expulsion. yHyppolite argues that this difference implies an asymmetry between affirmation and negation, indicating that negation is more complexly tied to the destructive drives. Not all negation, Hyppolite reminds us, is destructive: "to negate is more than to wish to destroy" (Hyppolite 1966, 750). Negation, beyond its destructive tendencies, marks the beginning of thought and represents what Hyppolite calls a "fundamental attitude of symbolicity rendered explicit" (752).

Hyppolite's insight can be further clarified by considering the logical behavior of affirmation and negation. A qualitative difference arises between them. As noted in the first chapter, doubling affirmation has no effect – it does not change the content of what is affirmed and is therefore unifunctional. In contrast, doubling negation produces a significant result: one negation cancels out the other, resulting in affirmation. This makes negation more complex and versatile – it is bifunctional, capable of producing different outcomes depending on its application.

Thus, while affirmation is a straightforward substitute for union (or incorporation), negation, as the successor of expulsion, is more dynamic. Like a descendant, negation inherits traits from its origin (expulsion) while asserting its independence, to the point of acting in opposition to its origin. This dual nature of negation – its capacity to destroy and to enable symbolic thought – highlights its central role in the development of intellectual and psychic processes.

This understanding offers a potential solution to the "philosophical problem" raised by Mosès: How does negation emerge at a stage dominated by the pleasure principle? The "hidden variable" missing from the earlier analysis is the *death drives*, which serve as the source of expulsion and negation. Freud reveals that the death drives are intertwined with the life drives from the very beginning, playing a role even under the pleasure principle (and can ever override it, as in trauma). This interpretation highlight that the death instincts, like negation itself, are not merely destructive but also crucially responsible for the development of a healthy psyche, generally being also a constitutive force within the psyche.

Thus, Freud continues, within negation itself – as a mental mechanism or series of mechanisms – two forms can be distinguished: healthy or "normal" negation and pathological, psychotic negation. The latter, which Freud identifies as "negativism" (1925, 239), reflects a "general wish to negate" or a pleasure in denial. (This term will be revisited in Chapter 6 on Green.) Freud explains that negativism arises "by means of a withdrawal of the libidinal elements" (239), which corresponds to the unraveling of the intertwining between the life and death drives. This unraveling can be understood as a result of the excessive force of the death drives: while the life drives are responsible not only for internalization and affirmation but also for maintaining the intertwining of the drives, the death drives, on the other hand, tend toward detachment and destruction. They manifest through mechanisms like expulsion and negation, but when excessive, they further disentangle the two groups of the drives themselves.

Clinically, negativism expresses itself through an exaggerated attachment to negation and absence, an inclination to detach from relationships through object decathexis, and sometimes a withdrawal from the ego itself, leading to self-destructive depletion and emptiness.

Expanding on Freud's remarks, Salman Akhtar offers a useful framework for conceptualizing negation:

> One begins to note that Freud's definition of negation is Janus-faced and might even contain two separate concepts: "benign negation", which enlarges mental contents, and "malignant negation", which diminishes them. The former yields epistemic benefits and thus seems to be motivated by

what Freud (1923b) termed "ego instincts"; the latter creates psychic holes and thus appears to be mobilized by self-directed aggression.

(Akhtar in O'Neil and Akhtar 2011, 7)

Freud concludes his article by emphasizing that, in its positivity, the symbol of negation allows for liberation from both the results of repression and the dominance of the pleasure principle. This liberation enables thought and action in the service of the life drives. He reiterates the clinical observation that "we never discover a 'no' in the unconscious and that recognition of the unconscious on the part of the ego is expressed in a negative formula" (Freud 1925, 239).

This conclusion, which ties back to the starting point of Freud's article, neatly reconnects the various threads of his argument as well as the sections of this chapter. Freud concludes his Odyssey by underscoring that negative representations cannot be found in the unconscious, on the one hand, and that unconscious content cannot itself be simply negated, on the other – in the sense that *Negation, paradoxically, affirms unconscious content* (Horn 2001, 93). Thus, when unpleasant unconscious material surfaces into consciousness – always in a negative formulation – its denial paradoxically confirms its truth.

Freud demonstrates that saying "no", while originating in the death drives, is essential for mental growth and the development of a healthy psyche. However, he also alludes to a darker, pathological side of negation: a destructive, and often self-destructive force that, like a shadow, lingers within the human psyche – and so, will continue to accompany the themes explored in the rest of this book.

Recommended Reading

O'Neil, Mary Kay, and Salman Akhtar, eds. 2011. *On Freud's "Negation"*. London: Karnac Books.

Hyppolite, Jean. 1966. "Appendix I: A Spoken Commentary on Freud's 'Verneinung' by Jean Hyppolite". In Jacques Lacan, *Écrits: The First*

Complete Edition in English. Translated by Bruce Fink, 746–754.
London and New York: W. W. Norton & Company.

Reference List

Brenner, Charles. 1957. "The Nature and Development of the Concept of Repression in Freud's Writings". *The Psychoanalytic Study of the Child* 12 (1): 19–46.

Freud, Sigmund. 1895. "Project for a Scientific Psychology". In *The Standard Edition of the Complete Psychological Works of Sigmund Freud*, Vol. 1. Edited and translated by James Strachey, 283–397. London: Hogarth Press and Institute of Psycho-Analysis, 1950.

Freud, Sigmund. 1896. "Further Remarks on the Defence Neuro-Psychoses". In *The Standard Edition of the Complete Psychological Works of Sigmund Freud*, Vol. 3. Edited and translated by James Strachey, 157–185. London: Hogarth Press and Institute of Psycho-Analysis, 1950.

Freud, Sigmund. 1900. *The Interpretation of Dreams*. Translated by A. A. Brill. New York: The Macmillan Company, 1913. Project Gutenberg, 2021. www.gutenberg.org/cache/epub/66048/pg66048-images.html.

Freud, Sigmund. 1905. "Jokes and Their Relation to the Unconscious". In *The Standard Edition of the Complete Psychological Works of Sigmund Freud*, Vol. 8. Edited and translated by James Strachey, 1–247. London: Hogarth Press and Institute of Psycho-Analysis, 1960.

Freud, Sigmund. 1911. "Formulations on the Two Principles of Mental Functioning". In *The Standard Edition of the Complete Psychological Works of Sigmund Freud*, Vol. 12. Edited and translated by James Strachey, 213–226. London: Hogarth Press, 1958.

Freud, Sigmund. 1915a. "Repression". In *The Standard Edition of the Complete Psychological Works of Sigmund Freud*, Vol. 14. Edited and translated by James Strachey, 141–158. London: Hogarth Press, 1957.

Freud, Sigmund. 1915b. "The Unconscious". In *The Standard Edition of the Complete Psychological Works of Sigmund Freud*, Vol. 14. Edited and translated by James Strachey, 166–215. London: Hogarth Press, 1957.

Freud, Sigmund. 1915c. "Instincts and Their Vicissitudes". In *The Standard Edition of the Complete Psychological Works of Sigmund Freud*, Vol. 14. Edited and translated by James Strachey, 117–140. London: Hogarth Press, 1957.

Freud, Sigmund. 1919. "A Child is Being Beaten". In *The Standard Edition of the Complete Psychological Works of Sigmund Freud*, Vol. 17. Edited and translated by James Strachey, 175–204. London: Hogarth Press, 1955.

Freud, Sigmund. 1925. "Negation". In *The Standard Edition of the Complete Psychological Works of Sigmund Freud*, Vol. 19. Edited and translated by James Strachey, 235–239. London: Hogarth Press, 1961.

Freud, Sigmund. 1926. "The Problem of Anxiety". In *The Standard Edition of the Complete Psychological Works of Sigmund Freud*, Vol. 20. Edited and translated by James Strachey. London: Hogarth Press, 1959.

Freud, Sigmund. 1930. "Civilization and Its Discontent". In *The Standard Edition of the Complete Psychological Works of Sigmund Freud*, Vol. 21. Edited and translated by James Strachey. London: Hogarth Press, 1959.

Freud, Sigmund. 1940. *An Outline of Psycho-Analysis*. Translated by James Strachey. London: Hogarth Press, 1959. https://archive.org/details/b2981487x/page/53/mode/1up.

Horn, Laurence R. 2001. *A Natural History of Negation*. Stanford, CA: CSLI Publications, Leland Stanford Junior University.

Hyppolite, Jean. 1966. "Appendix I: A Spoken Commentary on Freud's 'Verneinung' by Jean Hyppolite". In Jacques Lacan, *Écrits: The First Complete Edition in English*. Translated by Bruce Fink, 746–754. London: W. W. Norton and Company.

Hyppolite, Jean. 1979. *Genesis and Structure of Hegel's Phenomenology of Spirit*. Translated by Samuel Cherniak and John Heckman. Evanston: Northwestern University Press.

Laplanche, Jean, and Jean-Bertrand Pontalis, 1988. *The Language of Psychoanalysis*. Routledge.

Mosès, Stéphane. 2010. "Seminar. Freud – 'Negation.'" *Naharaim* 4 (2): 299–327.

O'Neil, Mary Kay, and Salman Akhtar, eds. 2011. *On Freud's "Negation"*. London: Karnac Books.

Rayner, Eric, and David Tuckett. 1988. "An Introduction to Matte-Blanco's Reformulation of the Freudian Unconscious and His Conceptualization of the Internal World". In Ignacio Matte-Blanco, ed. *Thinking, Feeling, and Being*. New Library of Psychoanalysis, 1–32. London: Routledge.

Saad, Amit. 2020. "On the Logic of the Unconscious". *The International Journal of Psychoanalysis* 101 (2): 239–256.

Chapter 4

Winnicott

The Negative Side of Relations

> A true covenant between us, an inseparable bind
> Only what is lost to me – is forever mine.
>
> (Rachel Bluwstein, 1985)

Donald Winnicott's groundbreaking and imaginative contributions to psychoanalysis have earned widespread acclaim. This chapter explores his unique role in advancing the theoretical and clinical understanding of the concept of the Negative. André Green argues that Winnicott possessed a profound "intuition of the negative" (Green 1997), though he did not articulate it as a systematic or explicitly defined concept. Despite this, Winnicott's body of work is invaluable in uncovering the nature of the negative and, along with Wilfred Bion's pioneering contributions (to be discussed in the next chapter), serves as a crucial foundation for Green's more fully developed conception of the Negative. Clinically, Winnicott's insights shed light on the intricate ways in which the negative manifests within the psyche, either supporting or obstructing healthy psychological development and well-being.

In what follows, I shall explore three distinct ways in which Winnicott's work engages with and elaborates upon the concept of the negative. First, I will analyze Winnicott's use of the prefix "not", as exemplified in terms such as "Not-Me" and "Not-Me possession", alongside his engagement with dichotomies and paradoxes. Second, I shall examine Winnicott's focus on the absence of the mother and the negation of her presence, considering how this absence can either facilitate growth or impede

DOI: 10.4324/9781003352853-5

it. Finally, I will delve into Winnicott's clinical observations regarding the psychopathological consequences of maternal absence. My discussion will primarily focus on Winnicott's exploration of transitional objects and transitional phenomena, as it is through their creation – or the failure to create or sustain them – that Winnicott develops a profound and nuanced discussion on the concept of the negative. In doing so, he offers a wealth of theoretical insights and presents compelling clinical examples that illuminate the centrality of the negative in psychic development and pathology.

Paradox and the Transitional Object

Winnicott's thought is suffused with oppositional concepts, which, as explored in previous chapters, are fundamentally mediated by negation. His work is marked by dichotomies such as those between child and mother, inside and outside, subjective and objective, creation and perception, the formation of an object and finding it as already existent, illusion and reality, among others. However, Winnicott implores us not to view these opposites as mutually exclusive but as coexisting – creating unresolved paradoxes that, rather than constituting a conceptual impasse, serve to enrich and deepen thought. In other words, Winnicott emphasizes that, in certain instances, the most fruitful way to understand a mental phenomenon is to apply two seemingly incompatible terms to it without resolving the tension in favor of one or the other. Some mental phenomena, he asserts, are neither one side nor the other; it is both at once. In "Playing: Creative Activity and the Search for the Self" Winnicott writes that paradox is intrinsic to certain psychic phenomena and "needs to be accepted, tolerated, and not resolved" (Winnicott 1971, 53). By delving into the fundamental nature of these phenomena – primarily transitional ones – paradox emerges as both their constituting, *defining essence* and as the way they are *experienced*. In the first sense, as Ogden explains, "opposites coexist [...] in a way that creates something larger than the sum of the binary parts, something nonlinear that cannot be stated in any other way"

(Ogden 2021, 842). This is why, according to Winnicott, "paradox accepted can have positive value" (Winnicott 1971, 14).

Winnicott's paradoxical thinking finds exemplary expression in the seminal chapter "Transitional Objects and Transitional Phenomena" in *Playing and Reality*. At the outset of the chapter, Winnicott introduces the concept of "Not-Me" to signify the child's first experience of ownership, embodied in the transitional object. But in other places, Winnicott employs the phrase "Not-Me" more broadly to denote the external, objective world. In doing so, he proposes that a fundamental oppositional relationship underpins the infant's experience of self ("Me") and the world ("Not-Me"). This opposition should be understood in three interconnected meanings: First, the term "Not-Me" signifies an *external* object that becomes needed because of the "aggressive component" of the individual (Winnicott 1975, 215). Second, as such, "Not-Me" indicates that the infant's sense of self emerges as that which is *different* from the external world – from what it *is not*. Third, opposition is understood as an *active process*: the "Not-Me" *resists* the "Me", with the world pushing back against the infant's spontaneous gestures or its will. Crucially, this oppositional dynamic – when it manifests as a constructive clash rather than an overwhelming impingement – is essential for the development of healthy aggression, which Winnicott regards as a vital component of normal psychological growth.

> The immediate conclusion to be drawn […] is that in the early stages, when the *Me* and the *Not-Me* are being established, it is the aggressive component that more surely drives the individual to a need for a *Not-Me* or an object that is felt to be *external*. […] [T]he aggressive impulses do not give any satisfactory experience unless there is opposition. The opposition must come from the environment, from the *Not-Me* which gradually comes to be distinguished from the *Me*.
> (Winnicott 1975, 215)

Winnicott explains that active-opposition-yielded-aggression – that is "not even organized to destruction" – "has value to the individual because it brings a sense of real and a sense of relating" (217).

By specifically designating *the transitional object* as a "Not-Me possession", Winnicott highlights a critical dynamic, as André Green observes: "[t]he object is here defined as a negative of me, which has many implications with regard to omnipotence" (Green 1997, 1072). The transitional object, as Ogden explains, "is not entirely experienced by the infant as his creation" (Ogden 2021, 839). The experience of the "Not-Me" makes the infant acknowledge his limitations due to the object's opposition and externality. This recognition that is derived precisely from the *resistance* exerted by the transitional object begins to erode the omnipotence that initially establishes the (illusory) unity of the mother–child dyad. Together with this, according to Ogden, Winnicott writes that the infant reveals a tendency "to weave other-than-me object into the personal pattern". This "quite remarkable wording", says Ogden, highlights something about the "texture" of the experience of the encounter with the transitional object: that although this encounter occurs in an immature stage of the infant's life, the not-me object is nevertheless *"being woven into what is absolutely personal to an infant who is early in the process of becoming a subject".* (Ogden 2021, 839, emphasis in original).

Furthermore, through this negative designation, Winnicott implies that the creation and use of the transitional object represent the child's first step toward *separation*. The creation of the transitional object facilitates and initiates the process of differentiation from the mother, who is now, in a sense, "negated" – that is, repudiated (Abram 1996, 350). Concurrently, the child begins to develop an initial perception of *difference* (as opposed to the identification that, until this point, has dominated its world) that results from the experience of separation that now emerges between self and other, child and mother.

Winnicott conceives of the transitional object as inherently paradoxical. It is, for the infant, simultaneously outside and part of the self; both subjective and objective; both "Me" and "Not-Me", just as it is both the breast and not the breast. It exists as both real and imaginary, both created and found. In this way, the transitional object occupies an intermediate, in-between space that serves to mitigate the pain of separation. It draws upon and symbolizes both the mother's presence and her absence, thereby embodying separation itself as a temporary, bearable experience – distinct from the perception of separation as loss. In this sense, the transitional object unites both the negative – absence, aloneness, and the space for growth – and the positive – presence, life, creativity, and the joy of living.

However, for Winnicott, "there can be no separation, only a threat of separation" (Winnicott 1971, 108; Abram 1996, 351). Thus, while the transitional object signifies separation, it simultaneously embodies *relatedness* and *connection*; it marks "the initiation of an affectionate type of object-relationships" (Winnicott 1971, 2). This assertion, which might initially appear counterintuitive – after all, hasn't an emotional relationship existed throughout the child's life between herself and the mother? – becomes clearer when viewed through a Hegelian lens. As we have seen in Hegel, a genuine relationship can only exist between *distinct* entities.

For the child, the transitional object – like the mother – becomes something external and other to herself while simultaneously remaining an extension of herself. The child creates the transitional object as something uniquely meaningful to her, yet also discovers it as already existing in the external world. It is neither an entirely internal object nor a purely external one (Winnicott 1971, 9); rather, it exists in a paradoxical space. It is both objective (perceived) and subjective (illusory and invented), serving as "one of the bridges that make contact possible between the individual psyche and external reality" ("Group Influences and the Maladjusted Child" 1955, 149, in Abram 1996, 341).

Winnicott places significant emphasis on the notion of creativity and the tension between creativity and perception. While a child is born into a pre-existing world, to transcend mere survival and experience a meaningful and fulfilling life, the child must continually create her own life and world – living as if she were the creator of the already-present world. When the child creates a transitional object by "assum[ing] rights over the object" (Winni-Winnicott 1971, 5), it appropriates it as "mine" and imbues it with affective meaning. In doing so, the child not only re-creates what already exists (as occurs primarily with the breast) but also transforms it into something new and unique – something that, in this sense, *had never existed before*. This is exemplified when the child invents an original name for the object. The transitional object thus becomes the child's *first original creation that is also recognizable by others* as such. This is so since it transcends purely internal, subjective form and takes on a material, external form that is nevertheless utterly personal. In this respect, the transitional object principally functions as the *primary quintessential cultural artifact*.

Moreover, while the transitional object may not yet function as a fully developed symbol, it nonetheless performs a symbolic role. It *stands for* something else – such as the breast, the mother, or the relationship with her – while simultaneously remaining a specific, *concrete* object imbued with unique meaning. Winnicott emphasizes that the fact that the transitional object is *not* the breast or the mother is just as significant as its capacity to *represent* them (Winnicott 1971, 6). In this way, the transitional object serves as a steppingstone, guiding the child toward the capacity to symbolize.

Recognizing the paradoxical nature of the transitional object, Winnicott emphasizes in the "Tailpiece" that this paradox "needs to be allowed and allowed for over a period of time in the care of each baby" (Winnicott 1971, 151), without being challenged or undermined. He warns that any attempt to resolve the paradox – either by asserting that the object is entirely invented by the child or entirely pre-existing in the external world – risks disrupting a vital developmental process. The imaginary nature of the transitional object must be safeguarded, and the question of whether the object has been created by the child or discovered in the outside world should never be posed to her (Winnicott 1971, 12). The rationale underlying this instruction rests on the understanding that by refraining from interfering with the "as-if" quality of the child's creative play, the mother's tacit validation renders the infant's imaginative act *real*. This shared, unspoken agreement about the meaning and use of the transitional object supports the child's spontaneous symbolic activity, thereby fostering the capacity for living a creative life (Abram 1996, 306).

Winnicott further clarifies that, in a healthy developmental process, the transitional object gradually loses its significance (becomes decathected) without the child experiencing it as a loss. As Adam Phillips aptly notes, "[u]nlike every other object that figures in psychoanalysis, it is neither lost nor internalized; it is not a substitute for anything else, anything prior, nor is it in turn substituted" (Phillips 1988, 116). This unique process of de-signification occurs under two conditions: first, the "good enough mother" gradually transitions from near-total adaptation to the child's needs to gently frustrating the child by moderating this adaptation; and second, the child begins to develop an interest in cultural activities and broader phenomena.

The role of the good enough mother is critical, as she enables the child to first enter "the realm of illusion" (Winnicott 1971, 14), and then, over time, to experience disillusionment and decathect the transitional object. Crucially, this occurs while the child continues to retain an intermediate, transitional, illusory space. When this space is successfully established and maintained, it forms the foundation for the individual's capacity to engage with cultural experiences, embrace the imaginative dimensions of life, and live creatively, thereby cultivating a deeply fulfilling existence.

Absence and the Capacity to Be Alone

The capacity to be alone is another concept that Winnicott explores through the lens of paradox. In the discussion that follows, however, I will not dwell on the paradoxical nature of Winnicott's ideas in and of itself but rather insofar as it highlights the roles of lack, absence, and the negation of presence within his theorization, with the aim of elucidating the broader significance of these notions. Winnicott regards the capacity to be alone as a hallmark of emotional maturity. To be alone, he emphasizes, is not synonymous with seclusion; an individual may be secluded yet lack the ability to truly be alone – a condition that often leads to profound suffering. Similarly, being alone is not the antithesis of sociality or the capacity for togetherness. On the contrary, these are complementary capacities, both of which stand in opposition to anxiety. When anxiety is present, both the experience of being alone and the experience of closeness with others become fraught and distressing. Conversely, when anxiety is absent, one is free to engage in creative acts. As the Israeli poet Natan Zach insightfully writes: "When loneliness is not dread / poetry is born" (2008, my translation).

Winnicott conceptualizes the capacity to be alone as rooted in the paradoxical experience of *being alone in the presence of another* (the mother or caregiver). This capacity is a developmental achievement – what Winnicott refers to as a "sophistication" – that depends on the reliability of the mother's care during the infant's early life. The mother's consistent and dependable investment in her child creates a protective, trustworthy environment, fostering the infant's sense of safety and emotional stability. This consistent maternal presence, which provides ego-support and reassurance, is eventually introjected by the infant, enabling it to transform solitude into not only a bearable experience but also an enjoyable and enriching one. It is in this context that Winnicott asserts the paradoxical nature of being alone: "the basis of the capacity to be alone is a paradox: it is the experience of being alone while someone else is present" (Winnicott 1975, xxxxiv).

The paradox of being alone functions in two complementary directions. Primarily, the child, while *in the presence of the mother*, is able to *erase* her presence and practice a state of aloneness under secure conditions. Winnicott asserts that "without a sufficiency of this experience the capacity to be alone cannot develop" (Winnicott 2015, 33). At a later stage, when the child trusts the mother's dependable existence and care, she can tolerate *her actual absence* for short periods. The internalized presence of the "good enough" mother-environment provides the child with a sense of company, allowing her to be alone – but not entirely so.

In the first process described, something particularly intriguing occurs. Winnicott postulates that there are moments in which the infant suspends, renounces, or erases the mother's actual presence while immersing herself in her own reveries and bodily activities. In doing so, the infant experiences herself as unaccompanied. Then, a space of *experience* is opened to which both external and internal reality contribute, where the infant can play, find herself, and become herself (Phillips 1988, 119). What psychic mechanism underlies this process? Although Winnicott does not provide an explicit explanation, he strongly implies that a form of negation is at work. The infant suppresses the immediate reality of the mother's physical presence while simultaneously relying on an unconscious representation – or perhaps a figuration of a primal fantasy – of the "environment-mother". This process, it might be suggested, exemplifies what André Green later terms "negative hallucination" of the mother. This is a *non-pathological* process, serving the purpose of psychic development (Green 1999, 190). Winnicott suggests that suppression can occur at an early, immature stage of development, prior to the establishment of reality-testing, due to the infant's creation of an "internal environment", which serves as a precursor to the "introjected mother", a more advanced developmental stage. As discussed in Chapter 6, André Green builds on Winnicott's ideas to develop his theories of "negative hallucination" and the "framing structure".

To sum up, Winnicott demonstrates that the mother's actual or imagined *absences*, as well as the gaps or imperfections in her adaptation to the child's needs, when enacted in a "good enough" manner, are crucial for the child's psychological development. These moments of absence and imperfection embody *the constructive work of the negative*: within these spaces of routine, short-term absence and minor disruptions, the child's ego is afforded the opportunity and impetus to strengthen itself, fostering the development of essential capacities such as defense mechanisms and symbolization. Totality, complete unification, and perfect maternal adaptation eliminate the possibility for psychic growth. On the other hand, an excess of such absences or gaps can overwhelm the infant, resulting in states of distress that may be experienced as traumatic. Once a certain threshold of time is crossed, the negative shifts from a constructive role to a destructive one. It is this predicament that I now address.

An "Existence That Is Negatived"

In "Transitional Objects and Transitional Phenomena", Winnicott examines how the absence of the mother or primary caregiver shapes the creation and meaning of transitional objects and phenomena, resulting in outcomes that range from normal to pathological. He explains that when the mother's absence remains within the infant's capacity to endure, the memory or internal representation of the mother persists in the infant's mind. As a result, the transitional object and phenomena continue to provide a tranquil yet lively space for the infant to experience itself and the world. The child can rely on both the internal presence of the mother and the comforting, concrete presence of the transitional object as a bridge of trust during episodes of absence. However, if the mother's absence exceeds the infant's tolerance and is experienced as a loss, the internal representation of the mother dissolves, and the transitional object loses its meaning. The infant is then cast out of the space of experience and reassurance into a realm of solitude, dread, and a sense of death-in-life. As Winnicott starkly puts it, when the mother is gone for too long, she "is dead from the point of view of the child. This is what dead means. [...] Before the limit [of time] is reached, the mother is still alive; after this limit has been overstepped, she is dead"[1] (Winnicott 1971, 22). Moreover, Winnicott argues that the mother's prolonged absence is incomprehensible to the infant and thus rendered meaningless. Loss of the object that is beyond understanding creates psychic void. When the child is unable to reconstruct or "resurrect" the mother's representation within its mental reality, "[t]he mother is no longer alive to the child (and I would add, the child is no longer alive to himself or herself)", Ogden explains (Ogden 2021, 844). The child's psychic reality consists of *nothingness*. That is, absence becomes the sole reality.

According to Winnicott, in such cases, "[m]uch of the material of the analysis has to do with *the negative side of relationships*; that is, with the gradual failure that has to be experienced by the child when the parents are not available" (Winnicott 1971, 21, emphasis added). Ogden provides an intriguing commentary on this observation. He contends that

Here, Winnicott is *reinventing the word negative* by means of the way he is using it. The terms, in Winnicott's hands, refers both to the failure of the parents to be adequately available to the child and to the psychic failure (damage) suffered by the child as a consequence of the excessive absence of the parents

(Ogden 2021, 843, emphasis added)

Ogden provides here further insight into Winnicott's concept of the negative, highlighting its nature as a *dual failure*. First, it reflects a failure on the parent's part to provide adequate emotional care, particularly in knowing *when* to return to the child after an absence. Second, it signifies a failure within the child's psyche to sustain the internal representation of the parent in a way that preserves its own aliveness and vitality. Thus, the negative emerges as the result of an excess of absence, shaping the child's inner world and object relations.

The negative, then, arises, to use Winnicott's language of paradox, from an *excess of absence* – both the absence of the mother in the real world and within the child's psyche. André Green expands on the implications of what Winnicott refers to as "the negative side of relationships". He argues that

the effect of these experiences [of traumatic separation] is such that it spreads to the whole psychic structure and becomes autonomous, so to speak, from the future appearances and disappearances of the object. This means that the object's presence is not able to modify the negative model which has become characteristic of the object's experience. *The negative has imposed itself as an organized object relationship* quite independent of the object's presence or absence.

(Green 1999, 5 emphasis added)

Winnicott delves into the psychopathology of the negative as "excessive absence" through clinical material, providing profound insights that cannot be fully explored in this brief discussion. Nonetheless, I will highlight some key points. Winnicott recounts his work with a highly intelligent woman to illustrate how "the sense of loss itself can become a way of integrating one's self" (Winnicott 1971, 22). For this patient, Winnicott observes, loss becomes the central framework through which her sense of self is integrated, representing the only psychic reality available to her.

For example, although the patient admits that Winnicott is better suited to meet her needs than her previous analyst, she remains emotionally and affectively attached to the latter. She asserts that the one who is absent – the one she has nearly forgotten – is "more important" to her than the one who is presently available. As she poignantly explains, "The negative of him is more real than the positive of you" (Winnicott 1971, 23). This statement encapsulates her psychic reality, where absence, void, and loss dominate her experience, overshadowing the presence of a potentially meaningful connection in the here and now.

This patient's history provides crucial context for her relationship with absence: she grew up during wartime and, at the age of 11, was sent away from her home and parents to a safer location, where she was cared for by foster parents. During her stay with the foster couple, she refused to address them as "uncle" or "auntie" and, in fact, avoided calling them by any name at all throughout the entire period. Winnicott interprets this behavior as "the negative of remembering her mother and father" (Winnicott 1971, 22). By refusing to name her foster caregivers, she maintained an unconscious defense against the devastating experience of loss through amnesia. Winnicott came to understand that this patient's strategy of clinging to oblivion – her complete forgetting of her childhood and her parents – functioned as a defense mechanism to avoid the pain of remembering what was once real. By repudiating what was present and tangible, she succeeded in avoiding to recognize the need for substitution. The negative for her was not only, as Ogden suggests, sheer truth – since the "replacement parents" were *not* her aunt and uncle (Ogden 2021, 844). The negative – absence, void, and forgetting – became her sole truth, the foundation upon which her inner world was structured. Winnicott observes that clinically,

> the important communication for me to get was that there could be a blotting out, and that this blank could be the only fact and the only thing that is real. The amnesia is real, whereas what is forgotten has lost its reality.
>
> (Winnicott 1971, 22)

The most intimate knowledge is the knowledge of absence. Absence becomes the object itself – one that cannot be mourned or worked through, for it is composed of nothingness. When the internal representation of the primary object fades or is blotted out, all that remains to hold on to is void itself – the sole constant, the one thing that is securely present and, paradoxically, impossible to misplace. As the poet Rachel Bluwstein incisively put this in words (cited in the motto of this chapter): "Only what is lost to me – is forever mine" (Bluwstein, 1985).

How can the patient lose what she never truly possessed? And yet, how can she let go of the only thing she does possess, even though it is nothing but nothingness itself? This void, made of absence, becomes not only her psychic reality but also her only emotional anchor, a painful paradox that lies at the heart of her experience of self and object relations. This is why the patient says to Winnicott: "All that I have got is what I have not got" (Win-Winnicott 1971, 24). As Ogden sharply explains,

> nothing is forgotten because there is nothing real to forget. Longing is not the emotion the patient felt when she was evacuated during the war. Added to the idea of "the negative" here is the idea that the experience of the negative involves both the feeling that nothing alive has been lost and the feeling that the nothing itself is what is alive and real. Let me put this still another way. The opposite of present is not absent, for there is nothing absent that is real: the absent never was present and cannot return to presence from absence […] *What is not recalled had not been forgotten. There is nothing to forget and nothing to remember because there has never been anything present that has felt real. The gap, the death, the nothing is what feels real.*
>
> (Ogden 2021, 844–845, emphasis in original)

Winnicott recounts a poignant detail from his work with this patient who, on a few occasions, had wrapped herself in a "rug" (a throw) that he kept in the consulting room. At a later session, the throw was in the next room, and although the patient was reminded of it and expressed a wish to use it, she ultimately decided against retrieving it. As Winnicott explains, "the rug that is not there (because she does not go for it) is more real than the rug that the analyst might bring, as he certainly had the idea to do" (Winnicott 1971, 22). He adds that this dynamic "brings her up against the absence of the rug, or perhaps [...] against the unreality of the rug in its symbolic meaning" (22). The patient's refusal to engage with the physical presence of the rug and her preference for its absence reflect a deeper skepticism about the symbolic reliability of objects and relationships. As Winnicott explains, when a child's transitional object no longer symbolizes what it once did – losing the reality it represented – it also loses its symbolic significance, which can sometimes lead the patient to question the very function of symbolization (Winnicott 1971, 24). The rug, in this instance, becomes a metaphor for the patient's mistrust in Winnicott's "motherhood". This mistrust mirrors her relationship with her own mother, who had betrayed her trust in an incident where the patient caught her lying, along with other experiences of perceived maternal failure. As Ogden suggests, the patient does not fully recognize Winnicott's presence in the transference. Instead, "he is, in the transference (and perhaps the countertransference), the negative of a real and present analyst" (Ogden 2021, 845). The patient, haunted by absence, separation, and loss, voices her longing toward the end of the session: "'I suppose I want something that never goes away'" (Winni-Winnicott 1971, 22).

In conclusion, Winnicott claims that for this patient, "[t]he negative is the only positive", meaning that not only is the negative the only thing she has and the only thing that cannot disappear, but also that by clinging to the negative or absence – the absence of an object – the patient turns it into something "positive", meaning a "last ditch" – essentially, a defense against losing herself completely, that is, losing her sanity (Winnicott 1971, 24).

A profound gaze into the agonizing psyche of such patients is provided by Winnicott in the chapter "Play: Creative Activity and the Search for the Self" (Winnicott 1971, 61). Winnicott describes a three-hour-long session. He agreed to the patient's request for a longer session after becoming convinced that "in a fifty-minute session no effective work could possibly have been done" (63). The patient sums up her experience of self at the very beginning of the session when she says: "'It's as though there isn't really a ME. Awful book of early teens called *Returned Empty*. That's what I feel like'" (58). This woman's general feeling is one of inner emptiness and nonexistence. She struggles to *become*, to solidify her subjectivity. At the beginning of the session, she is completely devastated. Her assertion "'I feel as though I came to meet somebody and they didn't come'" (61) particularly suggests that she does not recognize Winnicott's presence; More generally, it implies a constant experience of utter disappointment with the object.

However, Winnicott seems to recognize in his patient a hidden sense of self (or true self) that seeks to be found. In the first prolonged phase of the session, she is overcome with self-aggression, a sense of worthlessness, abandonment, disbelief, and nonexistence - a feeling that she "cannot bear to BE" (Winnicott 1971, 62). This leads her to exhibit episodes of *negative therapeutic reaction*: "I have a wish *not* to get well" (62, emphasis in original), she asserts. At another moment, she quotes from memory a poem by Gerald Manely Hopkins: "Don't make me wish to BE!" (62). Interestingly, the patient does not quote the line accurately. Like the patient's speech during the session, the original poem is filled with negatives and double negatives – which, nonetheless, converge into a fragile *affirmation*: an attempt to hold on to the resolution or yearning *to exist, to wish to be*. This is expressed in the poem's hesitant phrasing (achieved through the use of a double negative): "not to choose not to be":

> Not, I'll not, carrion comfort, Despair, not feast on thee;
>
> Not untwist – slack they may be – these last strands of man
>
> In me ór, most weary, cry I can no more. I can;
>
> Can something, hope, wish day come, not choose not to be.
> (Hopkins 1985)

The patient appears to hold an ambiguity about life, which is expressed as an internal tension between two opposing approaches. In the first (the negative), she despairs over the pain of internal deadness – emptiness, meaninglessness, and non-existence – longing to annul her very birth and wishing she had never been born. In the second (seeking to negate the negative), she clings to the "slack [...] last strands" of hope to be revived – by being reborn to a present and reliable mother (the kind Winnicott endeavors to offer). Both approaches grapple with the terror of "what is so awful", described by the patient as "existence that's negatived!" (Winnicott 1971, 61).

During the session, Winnicott offers minimal interpretations, waiting for the patient to arrive at her own insights, as "[t]he patient's creativity can be only too easily stolen by the therapist who knows too much" (57). Like an infant who needs to feel that satisfying eating results from their own effort, the patient must feel that the analytic work is her own (Abram 1996, 304). Winnicott provides a mirroring presence, allowing the patient to gradually recognize his presence and overcome her disbelief – and reluctance – to accept that she matters to him. During this process, she feels both alone and abandoned, yet she is also aware of behaving only *as if* she were alone in the room, acknowledging that, on her own, she would not speak out loud as she does in his presence.

A shift occurs later in the session as the patient and Winnicott discuss the vital need to be *reflected by another person* (as described by Winnicott in "The Mirror Role of the Mother and Family in Child Development", 1971). The patient shares an experience of looking into the clinic mirror and seeing neither herself nor Winnicott reflected back. Winnicott refers to a similar case in "The Mirror Role", where a patient, grappling with her sense of individual selfhood, says: "'*Wouldn't it be awful if the child looked into the mirror and saw nothing!*'" (Winnicott 1971, 116, emphasis added). Here (as well as in the previous example), it can be suggested that the patient is experiencing a kind of pathological "self-negative-hallucination", in which her absence in the mirror reflects her inner inability to perceive herself as an existent, real individual.

In response, Winnicott remarks, "*It was yourself that was searching*" (63, emphasis in original), immediately recognizing the ambiguity of his statement: she is both the one searching, existing through the act of searching, and the one being searched for, signifying her sense of absence. In doing so, Winnicott simultaneously acknowledges her as an agent and validates her innermost sense of nonexistence. He recognizes both her being a subject and her profound sense of emptiness and non-presence. This latter recognition, according to Winnicott, is vital, as it opens the possibility for communication with her true self (Abram 1996, 309).

Following this double recognition, the patient responds, "I'd like to stop searching and just BE" (Winnicott 1971, 63), and later, referring to a dream of a plane crash, adds, "But I'd rather be and crash than not ever BE" (63). For the first time, the patient begins to feel real and creative, and a desire to live emerges. Instead of being consumed by overwhelming negativity, she starts to move toward self-affirmation, where the "me" becomes distinct from the "not-me" and is emotionally invested. Yet, Winnicott notes that in the next session, he and the patient had to start over, eventually returning to a similar place where she could again partially affirm "the existence of a ME" (64).

Within the boundaries of the safe, reliable, and holding setting that Winnicott offers, he constructs an enabling primary environment that allows the patient a "desultory formless functioning" of the kind appropriate to her unintegrated sense of self. Unintegration (to be distinguished from disintegration which is a form of defense), a state of relaxation and trust, is necessary for play and creativity to develop – that is, for action out of genuine spontaneity within transitional space – as well as for a sense of being to be experienced (Abram 1996, 163). In this process, the patient must be reflected; she must feel found. Only then can she find herself and be herself, and only then can psychotherapy (i.e., interpretation) begin (Winnicott 1971, 54).

Note

1 This idea or, more accurately, what Winnicott refers to as "the death of the mother when she is present" (Winnicott 1971, 22) would later serve as the foundation for André Green's theorization of the "Dead Mother Complex".

Recommended Reading

Abram, Jan, ed. 2013. *Donald Winnicott Today*. Routledge.

Phillips, Adam. 1988. *Winnicott*. Cambridge, MA: Harvard University Press.

Rodman, F. Robert. 2003. *Winnicott: Life and Work*. Perseus Publishing.

Reference List

Abram, Jan. 1996. *The Language of Winnicott. A Dictionary of Winnicott's Use of Words*. London: Routledge.

Bluwstein, Rachel. 1985. "When". Ben-Yehuda Project. https://benyehuda.org/read/6660.

Green, André. 1997. "The Intuition of the Negative in Playing and Reality". *International Journal of Psycho-Analysis* 78: 1071–1084.

Green, André. 1999. *The Work of the Negative*. Translated by Andrew Weller. Free Association Books.

Green, André. [2002] 2008. *Key Ideas for a Contemporary Psychoanalysis: Misrecognition and Recognition of the Unconscious*. Translated by Andrew Weller. Routledge.

Hopkins, Gerald Manley. 1985. "Carrion Comfort". Poetry Foundation. Source: *Gerard Manley Hopkins: Poems and Prose*. Penguin Classics. www.poetryfoundation.org/poems/44392/carrion-comfort.

Ogden, Thomas H. 2021. "What Alive Means: On Winnicott's 'Transitional Objects and Transitional Phenomena'". *International Journal of Psychoanalysis* 102 (5): 837–856. doi:10.1080/00207578.2021.1935265.

Phillips, Adam. 1988. *Winnicott*. Harvard University Press.

Winnicott, D. W. 1975. *Through Paediatrics to Psycho-Analysis*. Basic Books.

Winnicott, D. W. 2015. "The Capacity to Be Alone (1958)". Internet Archive. https://archive.org/details/winnicott-capacity-to-be-alone/page/n1/mode/2up.

Winnicott, Donald W. 1971. *Playing and Reality*. Tavistock Publications.

Zach, Natan. 2008. *All Songs and New Songs*. Bnei Brak: Hakibutz Hameuchad-Sifriat Hapoalim.

Chapter 5

Bion

The Realm of the Minus

Wilfred Bion, a towering figure in twentieth-century psychoanalysis, is renowned for his profound explorations into the origins of thought, the nature of psychic reality, and the processes
that underlie the development of the mind. Specifically, he developed a distinctive and influential account of the mind's capacity
for both growth and destruction.

The negative holds a special place in Bion's thinking. It seems
he was profoundly aware of its significance, viewing it as a primary and irreducible aspect of psychic life, as reflected in his
statement in *A Memoir of the Future*, Vol. III: "Even the fetus is
involved with *non-fetus*" (Bion 2018, 58, emphasis in original).
Bion may have seen the "negative side of mental life" as the
shadow that inevitably always accompanies healthy psychic life. In
this sense, I want to suggest, he constructs an almost *symmetrical*
psychoanalytic conception, recognizing that every normal psychic
phenomenon or developmental path has the potential to go
wrong. Thus, Bion's writings are notable for their consistent
depiction of two opposing yet equally significant types of movement: one constructs and weaves psychic life, fostering the development of a healthy personality, while the other unravels it,
driving the personality toward a psychotic state. Sandler sees this
as part of a natural process:

> [P]sychic non-reality [is] an inseparable companion of psychic
> reality, in the same sense that the production of nourishing
> chemical products (such as ATP, adenosine tri-phosphate) is

DOI: 10.4324/9781003352853-6

inseparable from the production of faeces, or the storage of oxygen in the blood cells is inseparable from the production of carbon dioxide.

(Sandler 2018, 48)

Similar to Sandler's impression, I suggest that Bion never developed a distinct and explicit "conception of the negative" simply because the negative is inherently and ubiquitously woven into the entire fabric of his psychoanalytic thought.

Among Bion's most subtle and influential contributions on which this chapter will focus are the concept of "negative capability" and the concept of "no-thing" to distinguish from "nothing". Other key contributions, some of which will be briefly discussed in this chapter, include the following: absence of the breast or object; the minus sign; the "psy" category in the Grid; the "reversed grid" which represents a "destructive or negative force"; the death drive. As a rule, for Bion, as with the psychoanalysts previously examined in this book, the negative can follow either a positive path or a negative path.

Negative Capability

> If [the reader] isn't stunned, he is reading the wrong paper.
>
> (Ogden 2015, 76)

Bion's concept of "negative capability" is a striking example of the positive side of negativity. He uses negativity in the form of a suspension of desire, memory, understanding, and sensory perception to increase openness and facilitate access to the unconscious in order to reach, in the consulting room, the unexpected, the surprising, the new (Civitarese 2019, 759).

"Negative capability" was the first title Bion gave to the article that became his "landmark contribution" (Ogden 2015, 76), "Notes on Memory and Desire". Bion derived this phrase along with its original meaning, as is well known, from a letter written by the poet John Keats to his brothers, George and Thomas Keats, on 21 December 1814. In this letter, Keats was concerned with the question "what quality went to form a Man of

Achievement especially in Literature"? (Keats in Fusini 2016, 52). That is, what capability does poetry entail? (52). He seeks the kind of quality that "Shakespeare possessed so enormously", and his answer is what he calls "Negative Capability": "that is, when a man is capable of being in uncertainties, mysteries, doubts, without any irritable reaching after fact and reason" (quoted by Bion 2018, 125). Fusini explains: "As [Keats] describes it in this letter, negative capability is the *exact opposite of a wearied and wearying search to eliminate the negative*" (Fusini 2016, 52, emphasis added). It is rather an embrace and augmentation of the negative in the form of "subtraction, absence, and loss" (Fusini 2016, 53 in Civitarese 2019, 758) of knowledge, certainty, and clarity. "This formula", Civitarese explains, "is intended to indicate the state of mind that is most likely to facilitate an intuitive understanding of the unconscious emotional experience that patient and analyst are living through in analysis – what Bion terms the O of the session" (757). According to Bion, analysts should see negative capability as a "necessary discipline" whose failure will result in a deterioration in their observational abilities.

It is difficult not to recall Freud's concept of free-floating attention here. However, along with some basic similarities, Bion's concept presents significant differences from Freud's in its application and implications within psychoanalytic practice, which arise from the specific complexities of Bion's creative theory. I will first examine the similarities and then point out the differences, pointing to Bion's original contributions.

In "Recommendations to Physicians Practising Psycho-Analysis", Freud wrote that "The analyst should withhold all conscious influences from his capacity to attend and give himself over completely to his 'unconscious memory'". On the other hand, in more technical terms, he argued that "[the analyst] should simply listen, and not bother about whether he is keeping anything in mind" (Freud 1912, 112). First, both Freud and Bion share the same goal – namely, to facilitate access to the unconscious. The broad attention that Freud recommends encourages analysts to remain open and attentive to whatever emerges from the patient's mind, allowing for a deeper understanding of unconscious processes. Similarly, Bion's negative capability emphasizes the importance of being open to the unconscious, promoting a state of mind that allows thoughts and feelings to emerge without preconceived ideas or judgments. Second, both techniques advocate a kind of passivity in the analyst. Freud suggests that the analyst should listen without imposing his own thoughts or interpretations, while Bion encourages the analyst to fully engage with the patient's experience by implementing a state of openness that involves the temporary suspension of desire, memory, and understanding. This means that the analyst must refrain from the desire to provide skilful interpretations and, more generally, from the eagerness to cure the patient. Furthermore, it means that the analyst's theoretical frameworks, as well as the knowledge he has gained about the specific patient from past experiences, must be relinquished. Third, both approaches recognize the importance of the transferential relationship between analyst and patient. They emphasize the need for the analyst to be present and attuned to the patient's inner world, and to foster a therapeutic environment conducive to inquiry and insight.

However, the nature of attention that Bion recommends is also different from that which Freud suggests. Freud's free-floating attention encourages maintaining a neutral stance while listening to the patient, allowing for spontaneous associations to arise. In contrast, Bion's negative capability involves a more *active* form of waiting and receptiveness, where analysts not only listen but also *embrace uncertainty and ambiguity*, allowing for a deeper engagement with the unconscious. For this aim, analysts are encouraged to tolerate not knowing and to remain comfortable in a state of confusion or lack of clarity, which can facilitate deeper insights into the patient's psyche.

Second, Bion's concept of negative capability incorporates the analyst's subjectivity into the therapeutic process, recognizing that the analyst's own experiences and feelings can influence his or her understanding of the patient's unconscious. That is, the analyst's subjectivity is recognized as an essential element of the therapeutic process, allowing for a more dynamic and interactive engagement with the patient's unconscious. This contrasts with Freud's more traditional view, which tends to emphasize the analyst's neutrality and detachment. Third, in terms of temporality, Freud's free-floating attention, while focused on the present, does not explicitly prioritize the immediate moment, and often allows for a broader temporal context in the analysis. Bion's negative capability, on the other hand, encourages analysts to focus on the patient's immediate psychic reality. In fact, when Bion urges analysts to deny memory and desire, he is calling for a certain presence of the analyst within time and space: since memory is concerned with the past while desire is concerned with the future, their suppression involves a presence "here and now"; and since the former apprehends the "inside" while the latter the "outside", the negation of both makes, in a sense, the analyst "infinite", who acquires binocular vision or multiple vertexes.

Memory and desire, Bion argues, can be described as "possessions" that arouse greed and domineering behavior. Thus, when memory and desire are not suppressed, the analysand may *feel* that the analyst's mind is taking over or imprisoning her own mind. In contrast, when a state of mind of negative capability is created, the analysand's mind becomes unsaturated and capable of forming pre-conceptions. As for the analyst, her chances of approaching the truth of O in a way that facilitates the development of an adequate theory or interpretation become more likely (Bion 1970, 257).

Bion adds that both memory and desire arise against the background of sensory data, and therefore sensory perception must also be suspended, especially since it reduces the mind's ability to grasp the intuitive elements that are not discernible by the senses. Therefore, openness and receptivity are based on a voluntary self-blindness to distracting sensitivity to the external world, which creates sensitivity to internal reality.

Bion calls not only for the "the exclusion of *intentional* acts of perception at the pole of sensitivity" but also for "the exclusion of acts of understanding at the pole of the intellect" (Civitarese 2019, 769). He believes that a deeper exploration of the unconscious is achievable when initial forgetting, ambiguity, and confusion are present as a kind of "negativity" leading to new insights and understanding. Therefore, he advocates an approach of skepticism: the questioning, doubt, and openness to not knowing that are essential to resisting the premature closure of preconceived knowledge. Skepticism allows the mind to wander and explore beyond rational constraints. Thus, a negative capability encourages the operation of imagination and reverie that foster a creative space in which unconscious material can float in the form of "emotional pictograms and images. Not only because of their unsaturated, open, and ambiguous nature" but also because "this is the realm in which we see things from several points of view as well as in a complete, emotional, *and* conceptual way" (Civitarese 2019, 770).

Bion particularly emphasizes the importance of the processes of imagination and reverie in this technique. By engaging in imaginative receptivity, the analyst can "listen" beyond the patient's words and pick up on unconscious communication. He saw the unconscious not simply as a repository of repressed material, but as a dynamic source of creativity and insight. Through imagination, unconscious material – symbolic images, feelings, or ideas – can surface and be processed in ways that enrich understanding.

Finally, Bion argues that when memory, desire, and understanding are eliminated, the faculty of belief (F) emerges (while their preservation impairs its possibility). Faith, for Bion, is "*the* essential quality of the psychoanalytic attitude" (Eigen 1985, 326), the "positive" element that complements the negative capability. Bion does not use this term in its religious sense (which then becomes a saturated concept) but gives it a scientific meaning (which is not the positivist meaning of science but one that he formulates from psychoanalytic sensibilities). He writes that "for me faith is a scientific state of mind and should be recognized as such. But it must be faith unstained by elements of memory and desire" (Bion 1970, 32). Civitarese explains the connection that Bion posits between negative capability and faith:

> [Bion] points out that what "negative capability" defines in the negative sense – as Michelangelo says about sculpture, "by chiseling away" – "faith" defines "approximatively" (!) in the positive sense. If we think of photography, negative capability is the image that is latently visible only against the light, while faith is the photograph that is developed from it.
>
> (Civitarese 2019, 767)

Faith, not knowledge, becomes, in Bion's thought, the fundamental path to truth, "at once a method and saving moment"
(Eigen 1985, 326). It is the "something" that remains once the
"nothing" resulting from the withdrawal of desire, memory, and
understanding takes over the mind: an openness that is the
medium for accessing non-sensory and ineffable psychoanalytic
data, and is practiced as "alert readiness, an alive waiting" (326).
Faith thus enables one to accept the ultimate emotional reality of
the session, what Bion calls "O". While "O" itself is unknowable,
faith is the belief that "O" can be encountered. It reflects a confidence that meaning will emerge organically, even when clarity is
not immediately available. Eigen clarifies the difficulty that
accompanies this process:

> Bion describes how uncomfortable one may be in this open
> state. One must tolerate fragmentation, whirls of bits and
> pieces of meaning and meaninglessness, chaotic blankness,
> dry periods and psychic dust storms.
>
> (Eigen 1985, 326)

Faith allows us to deal with these painful emotions and move
toward the "intersection" of F in O with knowledge that supports growth processes. In other words, faith provides an emotional and psychological foundation for the negative capability. It
empowers the thinker or analyst to embrace the unknown and
the uncomfortable, trusting in the creative and unconscious processes that lead to growth and understanding. Without faith, the
ability to deal with uncertainty and remain open to the ultimate
truth ("O") will collapse under the weight of anxiety or the need
for control.

Like Keats, Civitarese argues, Bion is interested in the "intersubjective creation of oneself, development, evolution, of truth –
platonically – not as something to possess (or know) but as
'becoming'". Thus, he continues, "[The language of achievement]
belongs to the mastery of self, to an idea of life 'as of an initiatory
experience, that is an experience in which a second birth comes
about' (Fusini 2019, xxxvi)" (Civitarese 2019, 770).

Negative capability, then, consists of a dialectical interplay between the negative (i.e., skepticism, confusion, and unknowledge) and the positive (i.e., receptivity, faith, and approximation of O). Like the Hegelian dialectic, it gives the positive an advantage by *negating* the elements (memory, desire, understanding, sense perception) that *negate* openness, faith, creativity, and truth. Indeed, "[b]asically, it is a positive negativity" (770).

The "No-Thing"

Bion's discussion of the negative spans a variety of concepts and terms. In this analysis, I will focus primarily on the concepts of "no-thing", the minus sign, and the destructive force. Other topics, such as the category of "psy" in the Grid, while relevant, will not be addressed here. This section will focus on the developmental process of a healthy personality, with pathological processes reserved for later sections.

Bion's exploration of mental development and psychopathology integrates object relations theory with the constitutional aspects of human psychology. Building on Klein's ideas, Bion acknowledges the role of innate dispositions and temperaments in an infant's ability to develop a healthy personality. However, more than Klein, he emphasizes the critical importance of the care provided by the maternal object (or other caregiver) in shaping mental development.

Bion's examination of the negative begins at the earliest stages of life, rooted in the reality that a mother's presence is inevitably interrupted by moments of absence due to the demands of daily life. These absences evoke in the infant feelings of fear and frustration that are difficult to manage. The experience of the mother or breast being absent gives rise to what Bion terms the "no-breast" or "no-thing". Dialectically, "no-thing" signifies both the prior presence of the breast and its current absence. Importantly, Bion thereby emphasizes that, normally, the absence of the breast does not equate to nothingness or a void. Thus, the "no-breast" or "no-thing" is equal to the presence of an absent breast and the associated feelings of fear and loss when it is temporarily unavailable.

How the infant copes with this absence plays a pivotal role in shaping its developmental trajectory – either fostering the capacity to think or leading toward mental annihilation. The infant's ability to manage the mother's absence, along with the fear and frustration it provokes, depends largely on the mother's capacity to contain the infant's emotions, process them, and return them in a form that is less overwhelming and more comprehensible. As Annie Reiner explains, "[the] no-thing is essentially the presence of absence, creating a space in the mind where a thought – 'no mother' – can exist. The mother's emotional presence ultimately makes it possible for the child to tolerate her physical absence, or separateness." She continues:

> In the mental space of "no-mother" or "no-thing", the mother's physical absence can be experienced as a symbolic mental presence of the absent mother, a symbolic "mother" able to be held in the mind as an image, later a word, representing her.
>
> (Reiner 2023, 18)

Joan and Neville Symington, echoing Hegel, aptly state that thought is like a "negative" of an object. For example, when one thinks of a tree, the thought arises because the tree is absent in the mind. Its presence is evoked through thought, but this presence is like the "negative" of the real object. However, they stress that thought itself has a constructive function – it transforms the basic elements of experience into a meaningful pattern. Thus, they conclude that the foundation of thought lies in absence (Symington and Symington 2002). Reiner succinctly summarizes this idea: "Bion (1965) thus views absence as the essence of thinking, that a thing cannot exist in the mind unless there is a corresponding no-thing" (Reiner 2023, 19, emphasis added).

In his own words, Bion claims that "a thing can never be unless it both is and is not". He elaborates: "a thing cannot exist in the mind alone: nor can a thing exist unless at the same time there is a corresponding no-thing. [...] If there is a 'no-thing,' the 'thing' must exist" (Bion 1965, 218). The "no-thing", Bion explains, refers to "the place where the breast was". Thus, the "no-thing" does not emerge ex nihilo: "If there is a 'no-thing,' the 'thing' must exist". For a healthy subject, a meaningful object must both exist and be thought or represented in its absence. As such, it simultaneously is and is not. Hence, Bion states, "[t]he invariant under psychoanalysis is the ratio of no-thing to thing" (218).

The ability to transform the experience of absence into a thought forms the foundation for the evolution of a thinking mind. When the object is present, there is no need to dream, think, or represent it. The present, satisfying breast is, in Bion's terms (borrowed from Kant), "the thing-in-itself". The need for representation arises only in the object's absence. At this point, the "no-breast" becomes the first thought – a space occupied by "no-things". According to Bion, thought precedes and establishes the activity of thinking, just as truth, either known or unknown, precedes the act of thinking it.

Bion further explains that "the space occupied by a particular no-thing is marked by a sign such as the words 'chair', 'cat', 'point', or 'dog'" (Bion 1965, 221). The birth of thought, symbolism, and language provides a container for the infant or patient in the absence of the object. Language, as Bion states, "surmounts loss as it records the ongoing presence of that which once was" (221). This process transforms the negative into something constructive. Bion's thesis highlights the role of *abstraction* in this transformation. The concrete experience of the mouth encountering the breast gives rise to an abstraction of its properties – sweetness, warmth, bitterness, sourness, etc. These properties, again echoing Hegel, are "negative things" – that is, "no-things" that can be applied to other objects, finding "realization" in the external world.[1]

> From these sweet, bitter, sour objects, sweetness, bitterness, sourness, are abstracted. Once abstracted they can be reapplied; the abstraction made can be used in situations where a realization, not the original realization from which it was abstracted, approximates to it.
>
> (Bion 1962, 327)

This process involves holding together the emotional memory of the object (thing) – a capacity reliant on the object providing a "good enough" container – and the pain of its absence. By trans-forming absence (no-thing) into representations (no-things) or thoughts, the infant can engage with reality and seek a substitute object in the external world (Sandler 2018, 483). This turn to the external world reflects action guided by the reality principle. Spe-cifically, substitution occurs when there is sufficient similarity between the abstracted properties of the original object and the properties of the alternative object. In Bion's terms, the substitute object "approximates" the abstraction of the original object (Bion 1962, 294). That is, like the Freudian insight, he claims that the original satisfaction is irretrievably lost, and throughout life, one must settle for "approximations" – substitutes that are similar to, but never identical with, the original.

Bion's focus on abstraction as a negative activity essential for psychic growth aligns with Hegel's view of the "tremendous power" of the negative. On the one hand, the two differ in that while Hegel sees abstract thought as creating absence and separation, Bion views absence and separation as generating abstract thought, enabling further development. On the other hand, however, both agree that self-growth requires breaking from a unified whole and separating from the object (mother/world) with the mediation of symbolic language. The negative force of abstraction lies precisely in dissolving unity – for exam-ple, separating a property from its object. As Hegel vehemently states – and it seems that Bion could not have put it better – the ability to endure the "negative" (separation) and its accompany-ing terror, without fleeing or evading it, facilitates the mind's creativity, transformation, and development – and particularly, as Hegel also indicates, reaching (emotional) Truth. This is (as seen in the second chapter) the "magic force" that transforms negativity into "Being". I return to Hegel's words because of their relevance:

> Death, if that is what we want to call this non-actuality, is the most dreadful thing, and to hold fast what is dead requires the greatest force. [...] But the life of the spirit is not the life that shrinks from death and keeps clear of devastation; it is the life that endures death and preserves itself in it. Spirit

gains its truth only when, in absolute disintegration, it finds itself. It is this power, not as the positive which averts its eyes from the negative, as when we say of something that it is nothing or false, and then, finished with it, turn away and pass on to something else; spirit is this power *only by looking the negative in the face, and by dwelling on it*. Dwelling on the negative is *the magic force that converts it into Being.*

(Hegel 1977, §32, 18–19, emphasis added)

And then Bion writes:

An emotional experience that is felt to be painful may initiate an attempt either to evade or to modify the pain according to the capacity of the personality to tolerate frustration. Evasion or modification, in accordance with the view expressed by Freud in his paper, "Formulations on the Two Principles of Mental Functioning" (1911b), are intended to remove the pain.

(Bion 1962, 315–316)

For Bion, the ability or inability to tolerate the pain of frustration caused by the absence of the breast marks the *watershed* between a healthy or neurotic mental state and a pathological or psychotic one. Success in enduring this pain allows the infant/patient to modify it and transform absence into a thought, while failure to cope with it – and thus evading it – leaves the space where the breast was empty and destructive.

We turn now to explore what happens, according to Bion, when frustration cannot be tolerated and destruction seizes the personality. Bion's ideas on this topic are complex and nuanced. Within the scope of this discussion, I will provide only a general outline. However, before detailing the process through which destruction prevails and a negative force is created, I will first examine some of Bion's unique terms related to this subject.

The Point and the Minus

Bion's discussion of the negative is marked by two key characteristics. The first is his conception of the mind in spatial terms.

I choose "space" to represent, on the one hand, emotions which are felt to be indistinguishable from the "place where something was", and on the other, space akin to the geometric realization from which Euclidean geometry is believed to derive.

(Bion 1965, 237)

The second characteristic of Bion's discussion of the negative, unique to him, is his use of mathematical signs, letters, and analogies – such as point, line, circle, "beta elements", "alpha function", and the minus and plus signs – to denote psychoanalytic phenomena. This use of mathematical symbols is closely tied to the theme of absence. As he explains: "A mathematical illustration is afforded by the use of numbers for enumeration and record. An increase in sophistication marks the manipulation of numbers to solve a problem *in the absence of the objects giving rise to the problem*" (Bion 1965, 161, emphasis added). And then again:

What psychoanalytic thinking requires is a method of notation and rules for its employment *that will enable work to be done in the absence of the object*, to facilitate further work in the presence of the object.

(Bion 1965, 165 emphasis added)

Bion, drawing on Whitehead's history of mathematics, argues that psychoanalysis achieves a level of abstraction similar to mathematics. Just as geometry abstracts tangible objects or visual images into arithmetical formulations, and just as mathematics freed itself from counting concrete objects (e.g., using sticks or fingers to calculate $2+3=5$) by creating abstract numbers, psychoanalysis addresses objects in their absence – such as the "no-breast" ("no-thing") or the internal and external objects evoked in the consulting room (Sandler 2018, 447). In both disciplines, abstract objects become units of meaning, capable of being manipulated through thought in the absence of real objects.

A mathematical illustration is afforded by the use of numbers for enumeration and record. An increase in sophistication marks the manipulation of numbers to solve a problem *in the absence of the objects giving rise to the problem.*

(Bion 1965, 161, emphasis in original)

The ability of thought to represent things in their absence is central to Bion's theory. For him, this capacity is not merely a cognitive milestone but the foundation of mental life, emotional growth, and the ability to learn from experience. Through his clinical work with psychotic patients, Bion observed severe disturbances in the ability to think, symbolize, and process emotions. Without these skills, the personality becomes overwhelmed by raw beta-elements, leading to confusion, fragmentation, and, in extreme cases, psychosis. He viewed mathematics as an early human attempt to address psychosis, understood as the inability to think in the absence of concrete objects (Sandler 2018, 390).

Bion translates his spatial conception of the mind into geometry. He suggests that *the point* "may [...] represent the position where the breast was or may even be the no-breast" (Bion 1965, 199). While he also discusses the line (representing the penis) and the circle (indicating inside/outside), his focus remains primarily on the point, as will mine. Bion explains this choice as rooted in clinical observation, arguing that the emotional experience of the absent breast is transformed into a point (or spot).

> The point has appeared clinically as dot or dots, spot or spots ("spots" in or before the eyes is a fairly common phenomenon). I have described the point or line as an object indistinguishable from the place where the breast or the penis was. Owing to the difficulty of being sure what the patient is experiencing I resort to a variety of descriptions, each of which is unsatisfactory. The spot, for example, seems to be part conscience, part breast, part faeces, destroyed, non-existent yet present, cruel and malignant. The inadequacy of description or categorization as thought at all had led me to the term beta-element as a method of representing it.
>
> (Bion 1965, 196)

The point, as Bion describes it, is "indestructible, immaterial, and real" (Sandler 2018, 394–395). It is a "basic, elementary fact" (395) and represents what one must endure to think and grow. Failure to endure it allows the *minus* to dominate, leading to a psychotic state. The choice of the point can also be understood through its definition and role in geometry: in the Pythagorean's thought and in Euclid's *Elements*. Two main reasons beyond the clinical explanation suggest themselves for choosing the point to represent "the place where the breast was". First, the point literally indicates a place – it denotes a location, something spatial, yet it is one-dimensional and unmeasurable. From this perspective, it paradoxically both occupies and does not occupy space, much like the "no-thing", which marks the place where the breast was and is not. Second, just as the point in geometry is primary, foundational, and "atomic", being indivisible, the Bionian point can be seen as the starting point and elementary unit of thought. As such, it forms the foundation of the entire edifice of mental life.

In addition to the point, Bion uses the *minus sign* (– •, – –) to indicate the place where the object was. He explains, "For convenience I shall distinguish the object from the 'position it does not occupy' by signifying the latter by minus signs" (Bion 1965, 100). However, the minus sign plays a broader role in Bion's system, generally representing the "domain of the negative" (Sandler 2018). It is applied in cases where the links of love, hate, and the urge to know (L, H, K) are unhealthy (–L, –H, –K). These negative links reflect relationships saturated with emotions such as greed, envy, and jealousy. Importantly, the minus sign does not signify a simple negation or opposite of positive links, but, as in Plato's concept of negation, something *different*. Bisani explains: "[The minus links] correspond to a way of experiencing Love, Hatred and Knowledge in terms of absoluteness, and in terms of a radical impossibility of acknowledging loss, relativeness and absence" (Bisagni 2020: 818).

For instance, the negative of hate is not love but may manifest as "a gossip, manipulator, politician, or overly protective parent" (Sandler 2018, 313).

Bion's use of the minus sign – originally denoting negative numbers on a continuum with positive numbers, separated by zero – enables him to articulate a profound view: it is impossible to understand the structure and function of conscious and unconscious life without addressing the negative (in its broad sense, as used in this book). He thereby demonstrates that many mental phenomena can take either a positive or negative direction, depending on internal and external conditions. As he explains:

> I use the plus and minus signs to give meaning or direction to the elements they precede, analogously to the way they are used in coordinate geometry. [...] Whether (Y) is to be preceded by a plus or a minus – this will be determined only by contact with a realization.
>
> (Sandler 2018, 426–427)

For instance, "growth may be regarded as positive or negative" (Bion 1962, 70, in Sandler 2018, 426–427). Furthermore, Bion's use of the minus sign alongside the plus suggests that not only are different individuals placed at different points along a continuum between the healthy/neurotic and the psychotic, but that within each of us lies such a continuum – between the non-psychotic and psychotic parts of the personality.

Bion first introduced the minus sign in his discussion of K. For Bion, K denotes a link or relation of knowledge, not as a static body of ideas, but as the process of knowing – an effort to be receptive to and give form (however imperfect) to what is true in an experience (O) (Ogden, 2004, 291). Bion added this link (K) to Freud's two noted links, L (love) and H (hate). In Bion's system, K, along with L and H, is associated with reality, truth, and growth, whereas –K is connected to lies, falsehood, and distortion of truth. As Meltzer explains, while the positive links foster relatedness, the negative links reflect "envious anti-linkage, anti-emotions, anti-knowledge, and anti-life" (Meltzer 1986, 26 in Poey 2015, 41).

Bion focused primarily on –K, which will also be the focus here. According to him, "The earliest and most primitive manifestation of K occurs in the relationship between mother and infant. [...] In abstract terms it is between ♀ and ♂ (as I have proposed the use of these signs) [i.e. container and contained]" (Bion 1962, 356).

–K represents hatred of learning and awareness, which involve connections and changes and require tolerating absence and dependence. It is "not an absence of K but a perversion of the urge to know" (Fisher 2006, 1233 in Poey 2015, 41), "a constant attempt to show the superiority of misunderstanding over understanding; of misrepresentation over representation" (Sandler 2018, 426–427). –K "defends against emotional experience by attacking the mental linking processes that enable us to integrate thoughts and feelings, especially when such integration threatens to bring mental pain" (Billow 1999, 632 in Poey 2015, 42). Bion describes –K as "a cruel and denuding link of misunderstanding self and others" (O'Shaughnessy, 1981, 184 in Poey 2015, 41).

Life in the domain of the minus is harsh and devastating. Interactions are dominated by greed and mutual destruction. While K evolves from the transformation of "no-thing" into thought and fosters growth, –K develops when the "no-thing" produces a destructive force that, at its extreme, annihilates both objects and the space of thought itself. "If minus K dominates, then a reversal and perversion of what is healthy with what is unhealthy occurs" (Stevens 2005, 619); the entire mental apparatus becomes ill. Mental mechanisms, from sense perception to alpha function, not only cease to support thinking and integration but actively attack them. This is not merely a passive absence of growth but an active, often violent, assault on the mind's ability to think, link, and symbolize experience.

The Negative or Destructive Force

Bion's conception of the creation of the "domain of the minus" or the destructive force begins with a Kleinian foundation but ventures into new territory. Following Klein, Bion argues that the absence of the breast (the "no-thing"), which evokes a feeling of hunger, is perceived by the infant as a bad breast – the positive presence of a cruel "no-breast" (Symington and Symington 2002).

According to Bion, the "place where the breast was" has many of the characteristics of a hostile breast because it has ceased to exist. Stevens elaborates: "Emptiness is immediately filled with something, and since primitive fear and rage are felt in the absence of the good breast, this 'something' is bad" (Stevens 2005, 617). According to Bion, desirable objects that can be absent might be perceived as bad objects because their absence is tantalizing.

> The good breast and the bad breast, the one being associated with the actual milk that satisfies hunger and the other with the non-existence of that milk, must have a difference in psychic reality. "Thoughts are a nuisance," said one of my patients.
>
> (Bion 1962, 34)

Intolerance for the pain of frustration, especially when accompanied by strong negative emotions or a temperament that amplifies them, causes the bad breast to remain bad, even when present. Feeding is then experienced as emptying a bad breast out of greed and envy. The quality of maternal care is critical here – without the mother's containing function, it becomes impossible to think and find meaning in the feelings that occupy the space of "no-thing". The mind is overwhelmed with raw sensory and emotional beta-elements, which the infant quickly evacuates. In an attempt to escape the pain, the infant splits off its fear, projecting it along with envy and hatred onto the breast. If the mother fails to contain and return these feelings in a digested form, the beta-elements are charged with heightened frustration, fear, envy, and hostility. If the infant is overwhelmed by fears of dying, it will attempt to split and project these fears onto the mother, hoping she can moderate them. However, if the mother fails to contain them, she may strip these fears of any "goodness" or meaning, leaving the infant to re-introject "nameless dread" (Bion 1962, 362). This inability to generate meaningful thoughts leads to an underdeveloped thinking mechanism and reliance, rather, on projective identification. As Stevens explains, "the very mechanism for producing connections and meaning is attacked, and the world becomes a hostile, persecutory, and cruel place, blank and denuded of meaning". A force of "'without-ness' is created [...] [that] is the resultant of an envious stripping or denudation of all good and is itself destined to continue the process of stripping" (Bion 1962, 97 in Poey 2015, 41). In such a state, "omnipotence replaces the processing of thoughts and feelings, and omniscience replaces learning from experience" (Stevens 2005, 618).

When projective identification replaces thinking, Bion argues, "much more than mere fear of death is projected. In fact, it is almost as if the infant had emptied its personality" (Bion 1962, 363). A *reversal of alpha-function* occurs, leading to the dispersal of the contact-barrier. In this state, not only is the external world stripped of meaning, but the infant's personality is also emptied and bizarre objects (constructed from beta-elements combined with ego and superego traces) are formed (Bion 1962, 293–294). Furthermore, "The will to live, which has to exist before a fear of death can exist, is part of the good which the envious breast has removed" (Bion 1962, 363). As the Symingtons explain, the thoughts go *backwards* and become *non*-thoughts, but they acquire a threatening quality because of the hatred with which they were expelled. As a result, there exists a hatred of both mental and external reality and of anything that leads to aware-ness of them (Symington and Symington 2002). A "closed system" develops that "avoids reality and is characterized by sadomaso-chism, omnipotence, and stasis" (Stevens, 2005, 618).

Specifically, in this mental state, the infant/patient's ability to abstract and symbolize the breast as more than sensory "con-creteness" is impaired. "The abstract and general, if they exist at all, are felt to have become things-in-themselves" (Bion 1962, 364). In other words, the word is understood as a thing (Sandler, 2018, 125–126). Consequently, no representation of the absent object is formed, meaning it does not exist in the mind. At the same time, the mind fixates on what was materially present but has now disappeared. As a result, "'*without-ness*' replaces the real absence of something" (341, emphasis added). According to Bion, in this state, the object represents "no-thing", a frightening ghost, a damaged and emptied breast (Symington and Symington 2002).

Stevens explains that "an inability to tolerate 'no-thing' [...] amounts to a kind of murder of the mind, resulting in a state of stupor. This extreme solution to the caregiver's failure is itself intolerable" (Stevens 2005, 621).

When the bond between infant and mother is rooted in excessive envy or inadequate nurturing, it is internalized as a destructive "superego" that "denies the development and existence of the ego itself" (Bion 1965, 38 in Poey 2015, 41). This superego lacks typical psychoanalytic characteristics, instead embodying "a fanatical claim to moral superiority without any morality" (Bion 1962, 363). Its superiority manifests in "finding faults in everything" and, crucially, in "hatred of every new development in the personality, as if it were [...] an enemy to be destroyed" (363). Efforts to seek truth or connect with reality are met with destructive attacks and the reassertion of "moral" superiority (363). This internal structure, which is not modified by development, continues to exert a pathogenic power, attacking the links of emotion and reason between objects and contributing to the minute fragmentation and disorganization characteristic of psychosis. As such, it is a reversal of the Grid itself, a movement counter to the one that signifies mental growth, which Bion denotes by two arrows directed upward and left ($\leftarrow\uparrow$) – that is, opposite of the ones denoting a healthy development.

> The problem posed by [the reverse Grid] can be stated by analogy with existing objects. [The reverse Grid] is violent, greedy, and envious, ruthless, murderous, and predatory, without respect for the truth, persons or things. It is, as it were, what Pirandello might have called a Character in Search of an Author. In so far as it has found a "character" it appears to be a completely immoral conscience. This force is dominated by an envious determination to possess everything that objects that exist possess including existence itself.
>
> (Bion 1965, 217)

At its extreme, this situation leaves the person "existing in a passionless and meaningless hell – neither alive nor dead but somehow in between, surviving but not suffering" (Stevens 2005, 619).

Bion refers to this state as a "raging inferno of greedy non-existence" (Bion 1965, 247).

Samuel Beckett's "Lessness" is both a literary experiment and a psychological exploration of a state of mind or being defined by absence rather than presence – a movement toward the dissolution of meaning, structure, and identity. This minimalist fragmented text reflects the chaotic disorientation of an unmoored mind grappling with isolation, meaninglessness, and diminishment. Beckett's minimalist style evokes psychic disintegration and stupor, with its repetitive structure and random arrangement of words and sentences excluding an author or traditional narrative conventions. Words function as things – as disordered building blocks that are placed indifferently and rigidly side by side, reflecting a chaotic stream of (un)consciousness. The title "Lessness" encapsulates themes of absence, loss, reduction to nothing and less than nothing, mirroring the void-like detachment and fragmentation of catastrophic mental disorganization. It portrays a timeless, thoughtless, selfless mind existing in a passionless, meaningless state – neither alive nor dead, but suspended in a liminal existence. Beckett invites readers to confront the profound emptiness at the core of existence – a recurring motif in his work and, in this text, arguably also a reflection of the psychotic mind:

Lessness

Ruins true refuge long last towards which so many false time out of mind. All sides endlessness earth sky as one no sound no stir. Grey face two pale blue little body heart beating only upright. Blacked out fallen open four walls over backwards true refuge issueless.

   ...

Little void mighty light four square all white blank planes all gone from mind. Flatness endless little body only upright same grey all sides earth sky body ruins. Scattered ruins same grey as the sand ash grey true refuge. Four square true refuge long last four walls over backwards no sound. Never but this changelessness dream the passing hour. Never was but grey air timeless no sound figment the passing light.

...

Little body little block heart beating ash grey locked rigid ash grey only upright. Little body ash grey locked rigid heart beating face to endlessness. Little body little block genitals overrun arse a single block grey crack overrun. Figment dawn dispeller of figments and the other called dusk.

(Beckett 1995, 197–201)

Clinical Observations

In clinical practice, a –K link can manifest between patient and analyst as an attack, through projective identification, on the analyst's peace of mind, thinking, and reverie function. It acts as a defense against the emotional experience of understanding or being understood, which can feel hostile and threatening. In a –K link, patients lack curiosity, and Bion suggests they may benefit from being shown, through interpretation, their tendency to prefer misunderstanding and their disinterest in why they feel as they do (Bion 1962, 361). A patient may subordinate knowledge to the pleasure of destruction (Sandler 2018, 341). This is not the absence of knowledge but a knowledge of "truths without truth", expressed manipulatively, not to accumulate knowledge but to eliminate it (341–342). Truth, in this context, becomes a tool for pretense or concealment of truth, potentially leading to emotional violence. A patient will find it difficult to admit that the analysis is helping him and will insist, from a position of superiority, on a lack of understanding of the interpretations offered by the analyst or on their flaws, elevating non-learning above learning.

Bion highlights the importance of the analyst's counter-transference in understanding the destructive force. When working with psychotic patients, the analyst may feel as if his or her own mind is under attack, experiencing confusion, fragmentation, or even hallucinatory phenomena – direct encounters with the destructive force within the analytic field. The analyst's ability to tolerate and contain these experiences is crucial for therapeutic change. Acting as a container for the patient's unbearable emotions, the analyst must endure the intensity and violence of –K, "lending their faculties" and "dreaming the session" on behalf of the patient. Through this process, the patient can begin to recover the capacity for thinking, linking, and symbolization.

In light of the above reflections, Eigen seems correct in claiming that "Bion's writings contain the most detailed portrayals of anti-life tendencies of any psychological texts to date" (Eigen 1998, 33; Poey, 2015, 41).

Note

1 Bion's concepts of "definitory hypothesis" and "constant conjunction" are relevant here – a particular combination of properties that consistently appear together "produces" the desired object as a realization of the pre-conception/abstract representation.

Recommended Reading

Grotstein, James S. 2007. *A Beam of Intense Darkness: Wilfred Bion's Legacy to Psychoanalysis.* Karnac Books.

Sandler, Paulo Cesar. 2018. *The Language of Bion: A Dictionary of Concepts.* London: Karnac Books.

Symington, Joan, and Neville Symington. 2002. *The Clinical Thinking of Wilfred Bion.* London: Routledge.

Reference List

Beckett, Samuel. 1995. "Lessness". In *The Complete Short Prose 1929–1989*, 197–201. New York: Grove Press.

Bion, W. R. 2018. *The Complete Works of W. R. Bion.* Edited by Chris Mawson. London: Routledge.

Bion, W. R. 1962. "Learning From Experience". In *The Complete Works of W. R. Bion*, Vol. IV. Edited by Chris Mawson. London: Routledge.

Bion, W. R. 1965. "Transformations: Change From Learning to Growth". In *The Complete Works of W. R. Bion*, Vol. V. Edited by Chris Mawson. London: Routledge.

Bion, W. R. 1970. "Attention and Interpretation: A Scientific Approach to Insight in Psycho-Analysis and Groups". In *The Complete Works of W. R. Bion*, Vol. VI. Edited by Chris Mawson. London: Routledge.

Bisagni, Francesco. 2020. "The Landscapes of Minus: Hatred, Adolescence, and the Paradoxes of Growth". *Journal of Analytical Psychology* 65 (5): 818–838.

Civitarese, Giuseppe. 2019. "On Bion's Concepts of Negative Capability and Faith". *The Psychoanalytic Quarterly* 88 (4): 751–783.

Eigen, Michael. 1985. "Toward Bion's Starting Point: Between Catastrophe and Faith". *International Journal of Psycho-Analysis* 66: 321–330.

Eigen, Michael. 1998. *The Psychoanalytic Mystic*. Binghamton, NY: ESF Publications.

Freud, Sigmund. 1912. "Recommendations to Physicians Practicing Psycho-Analysis". In *The Standard Edition of the Complete Psychological Works of Sigmund Freud*, Vol. 12. Edited and translated by James Strachey, 109–120. London: Hogarth Press.

Fusini, Nadia. 2016. "Another Capability, A Negative One". *Italian Psychoanalytic Annual* 10: 51–60.

Harari, Orna. 2003. "The Concept of Existence and the Role of Constructions in Euclid's Elements". *Archive for History of Exact Sciences* 57 (1): 1–23.

Hegel, G. W. F. 1977. *The Phenomenology of Spirit*. Translated by A. V. Miller. Oxford: Oxford University Press.

Ogden, Thomas H. 2004. "An Introduction to the Reading of Bion". *International Journal of Psychoanalysis* 85 (2): 285–300.

Ogden, Thomas H. 2015. "On Psychoanalytic Writing". *International Journal of Psychoanalysis* 96 (1): 73–84.

Poey, Alan. 2015. *Bion in Practice: A Study of W. R. Bion's Work and Its Application by Psychoanalysts*. PhD diss., The Wright Institute, California. www.proquest.com/dissertations-theses/bion-practice-study-w-r-bions-work-application/docview/1729120060/se-2?accountid=14765.

Reiner, Annie. 2023. *W. R. Bion's Theories of Mind: A Contemporary Introduction*. Routledge.

Sandler, Paulo Cesar. 2018. *The Language of Bion: A Dictionary of Concepts*. London: Karnac Books.

Stevens, Victoria. 2005. "Nothingness, No-Thing and Nothing in the Work of Wilfred Bion and in Samuel Beckett's Murphy". *The Psychoanalytic Review* 92 (4). doi:10.1521/prev.2005.92.4.607.

Symington, Joan and Neville. 2002. *The Clinical Thinking of Wilfred Bion*. London: Routledge.

Chapter 6

André Green
The Work of the Negative

André Green, a prominent French psychoanalyst, one of the most influential figures in contemporary psychoanalytic theory, mainly influenced by Freud, Lacan, Winnicott, and Bion, developed the concept of *The Work of the Negative* as part of his extensive and groundbreaking psychoanalytic exploration. In an interview, Green identified *The Work of the Negative* as his most significant contribution to psychoanalysis, describing it as central to his theoretical and clinical work (Caldwell 1995, 30). The title of his book is drawn from the philosopher G. W. F. Hegel. However, Green emphasizes that his work is not rooted in philosophy but is ultimately directed toward psychoanalytic practice. While Hegelian influence can be found in Green's thinking, he makes it clear that "psychoanalysis has the possibility to reach the work of the negative without ever having learned Hegel", as evidenced by the British psychoanalytic tradition (5).

In Green's view, the negative is an essential and indispensable aspect of psychic life, so much so that no coherent psychoanalytic theory can be complete without addressing it. He asserts that the negative "is a basic condition for mental development" as it is fundamental to the process of becoming human. To regulate behavior, separate ourselves from others, think, and symbolize, "we all must say 'no'", Green explains (31). In this sense, the negative plays a constitutive role in the development of subjectivity, enabling differentiation, thought, and representation.

However, Green acknowledges that there are instances where saying "no" becomes destructive. In such cases, individuals may

DOI: 10.4324/9781003352853-7

prefer to say "no" to the object rather than saying "yes" to themselves (Green 1999, 286). Hence, they are trapped in a psychic reality dominated by absence and negation. Shakespeare's words in *Macbeth* – "nothing is, / But what is not" (Act 1, Scene 3, 141–142) – powerfully capture this psychic condition, which, as we saw, Winnicott starkly observed. Under such circumstances, negation ceases to serve its constructive, developmental purpose and instead becomes a force that disrupts and undermines the capacity for connection, symbolization, and psychic integration. The dominance of the negative in this destructive form, Green demonstrates, traps the subject in a psychic reality defined by absence, non-being, and decathexis. This destabilizes their relationship with both the self and the external world, resulting, among other things, in fragmentation and psychic deadness.

In the following discussion, I will first elucidate the meanings of the Negative or the work of the Negative as Green defines them. I will then outline the theoretical backdrop of his theorization by examining some of the psychoanalysts and concepts central to his work. Following this, I will explore several of the prominent psychoanalytic concepts Green originated and developed in his inquiry into the Negative, with a particular focus on its destructive pole. Finally, I will explore Green's concept of "negative narcissism" by referring Herman Melville's *Bartleby, the Scrivener*, followed by clinical reflections.

The Work of the Negative as a Meta-Concept

The Negative, in André Green's thought, is a broad and multi-faceted category in which the term functions not only as an adjective but also as a noun (Green 1999). As an adjective – similar to its use in Freud's work – it qualifies the nature of pre-existing psychoanalytic concepts, such as *negative narcissism* or *negative hallucination*. However, Green's innovation lies in treating the Negative as a noun. When viewed as such, the Negative encompasses certain psychic phenomena that are best understood as denoting the opposite, the reversal, or the absence of their "positive" – healthy – counterparts, like a celluloid film, which represents an inverse image of the positive. However, these are not merely simple opposites or absences but complex psychic processes that shape and influence mental life through their interplay with, or negation of the positive aspects of psychic reality.

Green emphasizes from the outset that negativity does not indicate value but rather *direction* – defined in the same sense outlined at the end of Chapter 3. Specifically, in Green's framework, to say that negativity indicates a direction means that it pertains to those psychic processes and phenomena that involve one or more of the following: (a) the act of saying "no" to something, (b) the failure, absence, or loss of the (primary) object, and (c) the withdrawal of libido (decathexis) and destructive mental operations, particularly those involving the operation of the death drive. Moreover, Green stresses that the idea that the negative does not confer value implies that the negative is not always bad, just as the positive is not always good. For instance, positive narcissism can be pathological, whereas certain forms of negative hallucination are essential for the healthy development of psychic life.

Green argues that the work of the Negative encompasses a wide range of mental phenomena and processes essential to psychic life. First and foremost is the unconscious. As Green points out, the prefix "un" signals inherent negativity, reflecting Freud's observation that it signifies repression and the absence of awareness, knowledge, and time. The unconscious operates latently, working "behind the scenes" of the psyche. Second, the work of the Negative plays a key role in managing the excesses of the drives by "negativising" them – binding, evacuating, or tempering their intensity. As Brunet explains, "Without this negativisation, psychic development proves impossible, and there is no chance of compatibility between possession and expression of the drives and being part of the human community" (Brunet in Reed and Levine, 2018, 114). This process ensures the drives are made manageable, allowing integration into social and relational life. Third, the work of the Negative incorporates defense mechanisms such as repression, denial, negation, foreclosure, splitting, and disavowal. These mechanisms share a capacity to negate – they involve the *judgment* of saying "Yes" or "No". Brunet describes this as the psychic process of determining "whether or not

a specific ideational content will be allowed to remain conscious or will be accepted or rejected by one or another psychic
agency" (114). Green frames this as a fundamental decision in
psychic life: a choice between "I agree" or "I refuse". However,
he emphasizes that agreement is not always positive, and refusal is not always negative. Acceptance can lead to pathological
outcomes, while refusal can sometimes serve as a necessary
defense or a constructive force in preserving and developing the self.
Finally, the work of the Negative includes phenomena tied to what
Green calls the "immense continent of the death drive" (Green 2005,
212). These phenomena – such as non-representation, decathexis,
and unbinding – stand in stark contrast to the "positive" aspects of
psychic functioning, like perception, representation, hallucination as
a way of managing frustration, and relationships rooted in desire and
physical contact (Green, 1997). This destructive psychic force works
against the links to objects and often turns inward, attacking the self
and embodying the disintegrative and annihilative aspects of psychic
life. These processes threaten the cohesion of the self and its ability to
maintain meaningful connections with others and reality, illustrating
the darker, destructive potential of the negative within psychic
functioning.

Aware of the complex and multifaceted nature of the concept,
Green makes an effort to clarify it by identifying several distinct
senses of the concept of the Negative, each reflecting its multi-
faceted nature: (1) The negative manifests as an active opposition or struggle against the positive, which Green refers to as the
"polemic meaning" of the negative. For instance, this can be seen
in the unconscious contents' struggle to rise to consciousness
against the resistance of the latter. This type of negative involves
a dimension of refusal, which, according to Green, may conceal
not only resistance to the object but also its destruction – a process that can simultaneously entail self-destruction. For example,
the negation of transference or the phenomenon of negative
narcissism. (2) The negative functions as the direct and equal
opposition to the positive, forming a symmetrical relationship.
Examples include negative transference as the counterpart to
transference love, or negative hallucination as the opposite of positive hallucination. In this sense, negative and positive stand as

binary opposites, mirroring each other. (3) The negative relates to states of latency or the interplay between presence and absence. Green draws on Freud's idea of unconscious thought that links two unconscious representations during free associations. As Green explains, "what is again not in the mind, that exists in a state of virtuality (and yet can be instantiated with the slightest hint) and that is absent, can be termed negative" (Green, 1999, 16). (4) The negative encompasses states of nothingness, non-being, emptiness, and blankness. It pertains not only to the absence of something that once existed but is now gone, but also to the absence of something that has never come into existence. Green distinguishes between what has died (something that once was) and what has never been born (something that never existed), noting the profound psychic implications of this distinction (17).

Green proposes the Negative (or the work of the Negative) as a meta-concept that unifies and encompasses all of the above meanings, even when they are different or seemingly contradictory. This comprehensive concept brings interconnected mental and emotional processes – both constructive and destructive – under a coherent framework, highlighting the central role of the Negative in shaping psychic life.

Theoretical Backdrop

A key milestone in engaging with the Negative in psychoanalysis, according to Green, is Freud's article "Negation" (1925) in which he argues that "negation is the intellectual substitute for repression" (Green 2005, 213). Green highlights Freud's revolutionary claim that the judgment of attribution ("Is it good or bad?") precedes the judgment of existence ("Does it exist?"), challenging the classical philosophical view that existence of objects precedes evaluation of their properties. In so doing, Freud suggests that the subject's emotional and relational evaluations precede intellectual knowledge. Green underscores this shift, noting that Freud moves from focusing on the subject's relationship to the world to its relationship with the other (32).

Freud also associates in this paper affirmation with Eros and negation with the death drives, identifying a pathological phenomenon called "negativism", a generalized wish to negate (Freud 1925) that results from a defusion of the drives caused by a withdrawal of libidinal energy, unleashing the destructive power of the death drives. Green builds on Freud's insights, exploring how defusion, negation, and the death drives manifest as destructive forces, central to his theory of the Negative.

Green draws from Winnicott and Bion but maintains Freud's emphasis on the drives, particularly the mother's sexuality, as central to psychic life. He critiques Winnicott and Bion for downplaying sexuality. He defines drives as "a concept on the frontier between the mental and the somatic" (Caldwell 1995, 27), and takes "an important step" beyond Freud by integrating drive theory into language, asserting that drives are both representatives and representations expressed through affects or memory traces (Reed and Widawsky 2018, 48). This integration allows Green to bridge relational and symbolic dimensions of the psyche with instinctual drives, offering a comprehensive view of psychic development and pathology.

Central to Green's thought is representation which he imbues with multiple meanings. He understands representation as a field of mental work that includes "three domains: the body (soma), the world, and the other" (Reed and Widawsky 2018, 48). Representation means, for him, "to make present in the absence of what is perceivable, and which thus has to be formed by the psyche again (Green 2010, 29–30)" (Reed and Widawsky 2018, 49). In other words, representation is an act of *re*-presenting: "at the present instant, in the absence of what I am speaking about, I represent (Green 2010, 29–30)" (Reed and Widawsky 2018, 49). His clinical work with borderline patients led him to identify *non-representation*, where the psyche fails to form representations, leaving the patient unable to process experiences. Non-representation, tied to the destructive Negative, is key to understanding severe psychopathologies characterized by psychic voids and deficits.

Green also emphasizes the interplay between drives and objects, asserting that drives without objects lack direction, and objects without drives are inert, and that the drive discovers the object, while the object, in turn, elicits the drive. He reminds us that every object is both invested by the drives and animated by its own internal drives. This conception bridges biological instincts with relational and symbolic dimensions, highlighting their co-constitutive role in meaning and psychic functioning.

Finally, Green extends Freud's concepts of investment and dis-investment (cathexis and decathexis), viewing the capacity to invest in something as an object in itself – created, sustained, or dismantled. This contribution is central to his theoretical enter-prise, particularly to his understanding of the negative's dual nature as both constructive and destructive – shaped by the inter-play of the life and death drives.

Building on the work of Freud, Winnicott, and Bion, Green charts a distinctive path, offering original insights into the psyche's intricate dynamics of negativity. His concept of the framing structure exemplifies his exploration of the dual nature of the negative – revealing how closely intertwined and entangled the concepts describing the activities of its two poles truly are. I now turn to examine this conception in greater detail.

The Framing Structure

According to Green, the infant's interactions with the "good enough mother", particularly during moments of physical close-ness, leave an impression of her arms or body or dependability on the child. This impression constitutes a *framing structure*, repre-senting the original fusion with the mother and is internalized to provide security regarding her love. As Green claims, "It is fruitful to think of the situation of holding described by Winnicott as a framing structure, the memory of which will remain when the perception of the mother is no longer available owing to her absence". This framing structure serves as "the platform upon which all future investments will unfold" (Brunet 2018, 116).

In the mother's absence, this framing structure works as a container, holding the loss of the maternal object through what Green describes as a *negative hallucination*. Green expands Freud's concept of negative hallucination, emphasizing its importance in psychic development. He defines it as "the non-perception of an object or of a perceptible phenomenon" (Green 2005, 218). Negative hallucination, in Green's framework, is central to the mind's ability to manage absence and create space for new emotional and mental investments. In a "good enough" environment, it allows the infant to "de-cathect the (fusional) hallucinatory perception of the mother", creating "an empty, potential space for the representation and cathexis of new objects" (Urribarri 2018, 70). Hence, it lies at the origin of representation; as Urribarri explains, "the negative hallucination creates a 'blank screen' on which the representational 'film' and figurative flow can be projected and framed" (70). This is why Perelberg claims that "it is against the background of negativity that future representations of the object are inscribed. This is the role of the negative in its structuring function" (Perelberg 2017, 52).

Green's perspective on the framing structure is encapsulated in his witty remark: "The psyche is the relationships between two bodies in which one is absent" (Green 1995, 69–70, in Perelberg 2017, 52). This statement underscores the central role of absence in the constitution of the psyche, a theme that aligns Green with the traditions of Winnicott and Bion. As Perelberg observes, Green emphasizes that such absence is not a total loss but rather "an intermediary situation between presence [...] and loss (Urribarri 2005, 205)" (Perelberg, in Perelberg and Kohon 2018, 51). It is within this transitional space – between presence and absence – that the psyche develops its capacities for symbolization, representation, and the ability to establish and sustain meaningful relationships, even in the face of separation or loss. In Green's words:

> The primary object becomes a "framing structure" for the Ego, sheltering the negative hallucination of the mother [...] the space which is thus framed [...] surrounds an empty field, so to speak, which will be occupied by erotic and aggressive cathexes, in the form of object representations. This emptiness is never perceived by the subject, because the libido has cathected the psychic space. Thus, it plays the role of

primordial matrix of the cathexes to come (Green 2005, 165–166).

(Urribarri 2018, 91)

This process can fail in two main ways: either when the mother's absence is excessive or when her presence is overbearing. When the mother's absence becomes too prolonged, the infant may decathect the object entirely, leading to psychic states dominated by "death, absence, and amnesia". The child is seized by overwhelming feelings of "solitude, helplessness, and despair" (Perelberg 2017, 52). The framing structure collapses, leaving the psyche unable to contain or process loss, thus disrupting the infant's capacity for representation and meaning-making. On the other hand, when the mother's presence is excessive or intrusive, it can create a "disorganizing, incomprehensible, claustrophobic internal and external world" (52). Perelberg describes this as a "traumatic intrusion" that prevents the necessary psychic space for absence, which is essential for the framing structure to form. Without this space, the psyche cannot develop a solid foundation for symbolization and separation (52).

A third way occurs when the mother is depressed, withdrawn, or emotionally unavailable – such as in Green's concept of the "dead mother complex". Then the failure of the framing structure may result in the creation of *psychic holes*. These are structural absences in the unconscious – tears in the fabric of the psyche (Green 1986, 146). They are characterized by a loss of meaning – what Bion refers to as no-thing – and a diminished ability to symbolize, represent, and distinguish between the intrapsychic and the intersubjective. Unlike repressed or denied contents, psychic holes are not latent but represent gaps where representation and affective connection have failed. Hence these holes cannot be filled by interpretation, as there is no hidden meaning to uncover; they are, as Green puts it, the *negative of psychic work itself.*

For Green, then, the negative plays a dual role in the framing structure, acting either as a constitutive force or a destructive one. When the framing structure functions properly, the negative (e.g., through negative hallucination) creates a psychic space where absence can be represented and new objects can be cathected.

However, when the framing structure collapses – whether through excessive absence, overwhelming presence, or maternal withdrawal – the negative becomes a destructive force, leaving behind psychic holes, disconnection, and an inability to sustain meaningful relationships.

Green provides a profound understanding of the destructive potential of the negative and its critical role in shaping the pathological dimensions of mental life. I now turn to examine some of his most prominent explorations of the negative's destructive role in psychic life.

"Negativism"

In an interview with Leslie Caldwell (1995), Green explained that, "in the bottom line", what the mother transmits to her baby while feeding him or her is the very ability to cathect, to love life, and to find life worth living. Freud, he noted, spoke of the instincts of life and love, and this vitality is what the mother attempts to pass on to her infant. The connection between mother and child is rooted in the mother's own pleasure in being alive (Caldwell 1995, 28).

Focusing on the work of the Negative, Green demonstrates how the pathological preference for the negative arises when the primary relationship with the object fails to convey both a love of life and a sense of meaning. When this foundational relationship goes awry, the development of mental life is disrupted. The subject, deeply disappointed and disillusioned by the object, withdraws libidinal investment from it and instead forms an alliance with the death drive.

Green refers to this state, borrowing from Freud, as "negativism". He describes it as a self-destructive negativity that becomes a closed structure – "shut in on itself" (Green 1999, 6). This state emerges from what he calls "a potentially creative negative" – a force that, under normal conditions, could foster the creation of a transitional object and space, as well as the capacity for symbolization and meaning. However, when this creative potential is distorted by suffering, rage, and impotence, it is ultimately transformed into psychic paralysis (5). In this state of negativism, the psyche becomes trapped in a destructive cycle, unable to connect, symbolize, or create meaning, leaving the subject adrift in a psychic landscape hollowed out by the unthinkable and unrepresented disappearance of the object.

At the heart of Green's understanding of the negative lie his concepts of *disobjectalisation* – that is, it may be suggested, the main form in which, according to Green, the death drive manifests itself. According to Green, when the infant faces a prolonged, unframed absence of the object – beyond their capacity to process frustration – the internal object becomes a site of traumatic impasse. The mind can no longer sustain the object as a representation, triggering decathexis, which destroys the lively and creative object within the infant. This marks the onset of disobjectalisation, a structural shift where the bond to the object is severed, leaving a psychic void. Disobjectalisation reflects a collapse in relational and representational functions, undermining the infant's connections to both the external and internal worlds.

Disobjectalisation is the reverse of the *objectalising* function. The latter, according to Green, is a manifestation of the life drive and represents its essential purpose (Green 1999, 85). The objectalising function is not limited to creating relationships with internal and external objects but goes further: as Green suggests, it is "capable, even when the object is absent, of *transforming structures into objects*". In other words, the objectalising function can "promote to the rank of object that which has none of the qualities [...] of the object, provided that just one characteristic is maintained [...], i.e., meaningful investment" (85, emphasis in original). Among these, Green emphasizes, even the very modes of psychic activity – such as investment itself – can take on the qualities of an object (85).

In contrast, *disobjectalisation* is a destructive process that operates through mechanisms such as decathexis and unbinding, attacking object relations and "all its *substitutes* – the ego, for example, and the fact itself of investment in so far as it has undergone the process of objectalisation" (85, emphasis in original). In this way, disobjectalisation goes beyond object loss. It marks a state in which *the very capacity to create objects* from mental activities is damaged or destroyed. While processes like mourning and melancholia still presuppose the existence of a lost object, disobjectalisation erases the psychic function of the object entirely – it *unmakes* the object. As a result, the capacity to create, sustain, or invest in objects collapses, leaving the internal world unstructured and devoid of meaning. This collapse of the objec-talising function represents one of the most destructive con-sequences of the death drive, undermining the foundations of psychic life and relationality.

As Urribarri explains, when Green argues that disobjectalising processes both stem from and enact the *death drive*, he thereby introduces a "fundamental change in the theoretical framework" of the latter (Urribarri 2018, 95). In this revised understanding, the death drive is seen not as an innate, ever-active force but as a potential that resides within the psyche. This potential is triggered by a failure in the relationship with the primary object and the resulting accumulation of unmanageable disappointment or frus-tration. When activated, the death drive manifests as an aggressive and destructive force expressed through decathexis. This destruc-tive force operates in two directions: outwardly, it targets the object, denying its importance or even its existence, and inwardly, in extreme cases, it turns against the self. In the latter scenario, the drive seeks to destroy not only the object but also the very source of the drive itself (82–83).

In cases of severe disobjectalisation, what remains is a *white screen* – a surface emptied of affect, representation, and meaning. Unlike a positive backdrop for psychic activity, as the one created with the framing structure, the white screen represents here the dominance of *unrepresentability*. This state reflects the failure of the psyche to perform the work of representation, which, as Green explains, involves both "an act of substitution for what or who is absent" and the creation of connections between representations that give rise to meaning (Green 1999, 86). When representation fails, the psyche is left unable to process absence, resulting in a void where neither presence nor absence can be symbolized. It is a psychic deadness manifested as apathy, emotional disengage-ment, and a profound sense of meaninglessness. Without the capacity to represent, the psyche cannot create or sustain relationships, leaving the subject isolated and disconnected. As Reed and Widawsky describe, in such cases,

> the frustrating and disappointing object is no longer treated as such; instead, it is a depersonalized function, a group of functions; it is, says Green, "disobjectalized". In the place of a libidinal-based object relation that contributed to binding, emerges Green's version of the death drive.
>
> (Reed and Widawsky 2018, 52)

A process related to this is Green's concept of *negative hallucination* which involves the *erasure* of something that is present and should have been perceived. In this process, going beyond repression or denial, an unconscious *disavowal* of the object's very existence takes place. Furthermore, unlike its function in the healthy framing structure, the psyche here not only fails to perceive the object but also unconsciously withdraws cathexis *from perception itself*. Green initially described this as the "representation of the absence of representation" but later abandoned the term due to its potential to blur the distinction between representation and perception. Negative hallucination can serve as a defense against unbearable psychic pain – such as the trauma of abandonment or emotional neglect – by "erasing" the missing object to avoid suffering. However, in severe pathological cases, it signals the dominance of the void, where "nothing is linked and no meaning can thus be discerned, where there is no meaning because there is no distinction between frame and content" (Urribarri 2018, 59). This contributes to states of derealization and depersonalization, where the object is not just lost but unseen, unregistered, and, ultimately, unmade.

Under the name *the blank series*, also referred to as the *clinic of emptiness* or the *clinic of the negative*, Green groups several phenomena that are clinically manifested as blank states, failures of memory, affect, or thought, and an inability to articulate experience. These states reflect a profound disruption in the capacity to associate or sustain connections between representations, resulting in a fragmented and empty psychic structure. The series includes conditions such as blank mourning, blank anxiety, negative narcissism, and blank depression. At the extreme of the blank series is what Green terms *blank psychosis* which is a latent, invisible form of psychosis that precedes the radicalization of the subject's self-enclosure (*repli*), where the individual shuts down entirely on themselves. In blank psychosis, "the action of the death drive 'empties the head' [...] the negative produces a psychosis without delusion, marked by severe disorders of thought, a consequence of the de-cathexis of the representational and emotional process" (Urribarri 2018, 71). The result is a *primary depression* of blankness, characterized by feelings of emptiness, total apathy, and voidance of thought. The "blank series", as Urribarri suggests, is elucidated both conceptually and clinically by Green's theorization of "negative narcissism" (or "death narcissism") (74) – to the examination of which I now turn.

Negative (or, Death) Narcissism

Bartleby, the protagonist of Herman Melville's short story *Bartleby, the Scrivener*, is a scrivener in a lawyer's office. His job is to copy legal documents and ensure their accuracy – a task the employer (the unnamed narrator) describes as "dull, wearisome, and numbing" – as it requires no creativity, only mechanical repetition of others' words. The way the employer describes Bartleby's initial appearance at the office door reveals much: "In answer to my advertisement, a motionless young man one morning, stood upon my office threshold [...] I can see that figure now, pallidly neat, pitiably respectable, incurably forlorn! It was Bartleby" (Melville 1853, 10)

Bartleby is a pale, corpse-like, passive – if not static – man who is withdrawn and reclusive. While he initially copies documents with great efficiency, at a certain point, he ceases not only to copy but also to be of any use to his employer in any other way. For hours, he stands and gazes at the "dead wall" – as though staring into his own future. In the end, his employer finds him dead in prison, "strangely huddled at the base of the wall, his knees drawn up, and lying on his side, his head touching the cold stones" (38).

We know almost nothing positive about Bartleby. Where did he come from? Does he have, or did he ever have, a family? Bartleby is a silent, immobile man; a "fixture", "quiet as one of the old chairs", a "shipwreck", seeking to be "anchored in one place". And yet, he stands firm in his resolve: "I would prefer not to", he repeatedly says. He insists on his desire not to desire, not to act, and not to reveal anything about himself.

Melville describes Bartleby as "more a man of preferences than assumptions" (26); his resolute preference does not refer to any specific thing but to the very possibility of preferring. Bartleby prefers not to prefer anything: not to copy, not to move from his place, not to relocate, not to take what is given to him, not to make any change, and, in the end, not even to eat.

Jean-Bertrand Pontalis, in his essay "The Negative Affirmation" (*L'affirmation negative*) (2000) explores Melville's *Bartleby* as a profound literary figure embodying the paradox of negation and refusal. Pontalis interprets Bartleby as a symbol of resistance through passivity – a character who refuses the demands and expectations imposed by the world around him. Bartleby's repeated phrase, "I would prefer not to", becomes a powerful expression of negation – not as outright rebellion or defiance, but as a quiet, immovable stance. Bartleby, it can be suggested, quietly affirms nothing but negation itself. By refusing to engage with the demands of life, he does not assert a will to oppose but instead *negates the idea of will itself.* His passivity is absolute, extending to all aspects of existence, including work, movement, and even basic survival. Pontalis highlights how this refusal destabilizes those around Bartleby, particularly the narrator, who struggles to make sense of Bartleby's behavior and is deeply unsettled by this enigmatic figure.

Pontalis sees Bartleby's refusal as an existential and philosophical gesture. For him, Bartleby's "negative affirmation" is not merely an act of rejection but a quiet declaration of autonomy. It is a refusal to conform to societal expectations, participate in the mechanisms of productivity, or engage in the conventional dynamics of human interaction. Bartleby's negation, then, becomes both a form of liberation and a kind of self-erasure, as his persistent refusal ultimately leads to his complete withdrawal from life as well as to self-draining.

Bartleby is the living dead. He rejects, avoids, abandons, and relinquishes. He wants nothing and chooses nothingness. Bartleby is a man in freefall, unable to halt his endless decline. A man without salvation, as Melville describes him – not because there is no one willing to extend a hand and help him, but because Bartleby is incapable of accepting help or redemption. In light of this, I propose that Bartleby's behavior exemplifies what André Green terms "negative narcissism".

Green distinguishes between *positive narcissism*, which aims for "unity, a narcissism directed toward 'oneness' – an investment in the self that is nourished, at least partially, at the expense of investment in the object", and *negative narcissism*, which "strives toward zero, is directed toward nothingness, and moves toward psychic death". Negative narcissism, Green explains, "is aimed at the self-depletion of the subject, almost to the point of self-annihilation" (Green 2002, 637).

Bartleby's behavior discloses the "ruthless logic of despair" (Pontalis 2000) and, as such, strongly articulates the Negative. In the concept of "negative narcissism", Green ties together Freud's separate ideas of narcissism and the death drive. The death drive, as Freud originally stated, is repetitive in essence, and this is clearly demonstrated through Bartleby's recurring statement, which expresses his singular and resolute claim to the right to want nothing. Repetition is shown here to be self-annihilating – culminating in the total destitution of Bartleby's personality. Bartleby's negative narcissism is exemplified through complete decathexis – the removal of emotional or psychic investment from his work, from others, and eventually from himself and life itself. Green refers to this phenomenon as "anorexia of life". Bartleby seems to disobjectalize not only internal objects but also the very object of investing. Hence, he becomes inert, a stupor. He uncouples, one by one, all ties to reality and to others, unable to revive his internal objects, his ego is impoverished and ultimately decathected.

Support for the claim that Bartleby personifies negative narcissism can be found in the case study Green presents to illustrate this concept, that exhibits similarities to Bartleby's case. Green describes his treatment of Mrs. Y, who was hospitalized due to severe depression in which she was deeply immersed. Whereas doctors' attempts to help her using a variety of biological treatments failed, she was eventually referred to Green. Green recalls the first time he saw Mrs. Y: "She sat before me, her head bent toward her chest, not daring to look at me, speaking in a faint voice, undoubtedly immersed in deep sorrow." Interestingly, there are several significant parallels between Mrs. Y and Bartleby. Mrs. Y was a philosophy lecturer but left teaching after just one academic year. She was convinced she was "the worst lecturer that ever existed". Her "guilt" stemmed from the fact that she "merely taught [philosophy], relying on books written by others" rather than "inventing philosophy, as Socrates did" (Green 2002, 641).

When psychoanalytic treatment began, Mrs. Y did not leave her apartment except to attend sessions, nor did she socialize with friends. She received a small stipend due to her inability to work and lived very modestly. She never prepared meals for herself and subsisted solely on sausage and yogurt (641–642). According to Green, the therapy sessions "seemed repetitive and sterile; no insights emerged. No changes occurred." Green admits he "felt pity and compassion for her suffering". Her sudden and mysterious death occurred – paradoxically reversing the self-starvation that ultimately claims Bartleby – when she attempted to consume a large quantity of food and choked to death.

Green argues that while Mrs. Y's case could be seen as one of chronic depression, he prefers to view it as an instance of negative narcissism, "characterized by a persistent aspiration toward nothingness". He justifies this position by noting that throughout his treatment of Mrs. Y, he found no evidence of her investing in any external objects, aside from himself – not as an analyst, but as a person, he emphasizes. Mrs. Y told Green about a car accident she was in and said that while waiting for the ambulance, she thought of only one person: him. According to Green, Mrs. Y splits her transference between the object as a person and the object as an analyst. She does not expect a return of love or the establishment of transferential and countertransferential relationships (645). Moreover, Green states:

She loved me, but she could not use anything I could offer her – and in particular, she was unable to gain understanding of her mental world. Her friends, who tried to help her, quickly gave up and abandoned her. I must admit that I failed to help her, though I understood that my becoming an object of love for her was an important step that ensured her survival for a while.

(Green 2002, 643)

Interestingly, Bartleby seems to be similarly attached to his employer – he "prefers not to" leave him – if only so that he may serve as a *witness* that will validate his self-experience, his devastating journey toward death (Amir 2013). He stops eating and dies shortly after his employer renounces him.

Bartleby, it may be suggested, desires not to desire – a stance which challenges the foundations of psychic life. Desire is essential to the psyche, driving relationships, creativity, and self-realization. To desire is to engage with the world, recognize lack, and pursue fulfillment. Refusing to desire, the will not to will anything, signifies a radical withdrawal from life and a denial of the internal drive to seek and act. It is a stance of self-negation, manifesting as profound passivity, where the subject refuses to participate in life whatsoever. This refusal leads to psychic stasis, abandoning the tension between desire and reality. While it may seem autonomous or resistant, the refusal to desire undermines the processes sustaining psychic life, resulting in immobility and self-impoverishment. The self retreats into a void, collapsing into nothingness. Bartleby's passive refusal exemplifies this tension between autonomy and annihilation, presence and absence, as his self becomes increasingly thing-like.

Pontalis and Green argue that such patients are often regarded as untreatable and incurable because they refuse to surrender to the life drive. Instead, they cling to the death drive in unrelenting loneliness. These patients exhibit a *negative therapeutic reaction* or *negative transference* that touches the core of the Negative: for them, renouncing psychic pain does not signify living but dying. Consequently, they cannot allow themselves to improve. They remain desperately attached to their pain, as it is the only internal "object" that exists within their desolate psyche. This "object" cannot be relinquished, as doing so would mean losing their sense of self and plunging into meaningless nothingness – a void. Existing as "dead alive" becomes their sole means of survival. Whereas, in Bartleby's case, pure negativity – death itself – eventually consumes him. As Green writes: "*Death narcissism* is a culture of void, emptiness, self-contempt, destructive withdrawal, and permanent self-depreciation with a predominant masochistic quality: tears, tears, tears" (Green 2002, 645).

Bartleby's obstinacy, it seems, drives those around him – as well as the reader of his story – mad. Yet, as Pontalis observes, there is something disturbingly fascinating about the way Mellvil depicts Bartleby drifting inexorably toward his own death.

Clinical Reflections

"One of the most tenacious forms of resistance" encountered in psychoanalysis, Green observes, is primary depression, that may manifest as a *negative hallucination of thought*, where thought itself is erased or rendered unperceivable. This resistance is so persistent, precisely because it involves the very psychic processes necessary for analysis to unfold. Clinically, it is expressed, for example thus:

> patients [...] do not acknowledge, even after the analyst has given precise circumstantial details, having said such and such a thing, or having accepted the interpretation which was given of it and which was recognized as truth at the moment when the material was interpreted [...] it is as though there is a real dissociation between the sonority of words and their conscious meaning on the one hand, and their unconscious meaning as it has been presented by the interpretation, on the other.
>
> (Green 2005, 220)

Another clinical challenge in cases of blank psychosis is the patients' inability to use the analytic setting. This predicament, Green argues, requires the analyst "to understand the meaning of the setting itself (Green 1975, 10)" (Reed and Widawsky 2018, 53). Reed and Widawsky explain that such patients "need help recognizing what they experience and feel", hence the analyst must rely on countertransference to articulate what these patients experience but cannot express (55). The analyst must engage with "a world [...] which requires imagination from him (Green 1975, 10)" and transform the inner states evoked within him into words (Reed and Widawsky in Reed and Levine, 2018, 54).

To address this, Green introduces the concept of "the virtual", which he links to tertiary processes. This idea is closely related to Bion's concept of "negative capability", which Green views as "the most fruitful and creative form of the work of the negative" (Green 2005 in Urribarri 2018, 83). The virtual refers to the analyst's ability to offer interpretations that depend on

> working through, which is an activity with a delayed effect (*après-coup*). [Therefore] it is best for it to emerge as an aperture of the latency in which it was being kept. At that moment we see a kind of "positivation" of the negative or transformation of the negative into the virtual. With this precise movement, the [analyst's] unarticulated unconscious thought is articulated when it is spoken and accesses the level of language.
>
> (Green 2005 in Urribarri 2018, 83)

The analyst's psychic work in these situations can be understood through Green's concept of the "internal setting/frame", which integrates evenly suspended attention, countertransference, and analytic imagination, while emphasizing the role of tertiary processes in listening and interpretation. Urribarri explains that the analyst needs "a maximum of psychical vitality and creativity to sustain and overcome situations at the limit of analysability – those in which the unrepresentable destructivity dominates the transference scene" (Urribarri 2018, 83). The analyst's ability to remain open to the negative and transform it into meaning is therefore central to the analytic process.

Green's idea of the limits of analysability does not depend on the patient's diagnosis but rather on "the possibilities of the patient-analyst couple to institute a setting, establish an analytic relation, and create an analytic object" (73). These possibilities hinge on the patient's representational capacity and the analyst's "analytic imagination (figurability) and working through of countertransference" (73). This relational and imaginative dynamic is essential for transforming the unrepresentable into something that can be articulated, symbolized, and worked through.

Recommended Reading

Kohon, Gregorio, ed. 1999. *The Dead Mother: The Work of André Green*. Routledge.

Perelberg, Rosine Jozef, and Gregorio Kohon, eds. 2017. *The Greening of Psychoanalysis: André Green's New Paradigm in Contemporary Theory and Practice*. Karnac.

Reed, Gail S., and Howard B. Levine, eds. 2018. *André Green Revisited: Representation and the Work of the Negative*. Routledge.

Reference List

Amir, Dana. 2013. *Cleft Tongue*. Jerusalem: Magnes Press.

Brunet, Marie France. 2018. "Thought and the Work of the Negative". In *André Green Revisited: Representation and the Work of the Negative*. Edited by Gail S. Reed and Howard B. Levine. London: Routledge.

Caldwell, Lesley. 1995. "An Interview with André Green". *New Formations* 1995 (26).

Freud, Sigmund. 1925. "Negation". In *The Standard Edition of the Complete Psychological Works of Sigmund Freud*, Vol. 19. Edited and translated by James Strachey, 235–239. London: Hogarth Press, 1961.

Green, André. 1986. "The Dead Mother". In *On Private Madness*. London: Hogarth Press.

Green, André. 1997. "The Intuition of the Negative in Playing and Reality". *International Journal of Psycho-Analysis* 78: 1071–1084.

Green, André. 1999. *The Work of the Negative*. London: Free Association Books.

Green, André. 2001. *Life Narcissism, Death Narcissism*. Translated by Andrew Weller. London and New York: Free Association Books.

Green, André. 2002. "A Dual Conception of Narcissism: Positive and Negative Organizations". *Psychoanalytic Quarterly* 71: 631–649.

Green, André. 2005. *Key Ideas for a Contemporary Psychoanalysis: Misrecognition and Recognition of the Unconscious.* Translated by Andrew Weller. London: Routledge.

Melville, Herman. 1853. *Bartleby, The Scrivener.* Alice & Books. www.aliceandbooks.com/book/bartleby-the-scrivener/herman-melville/454.

Perelberg, Rosine Jozef. 2017. "Negative Hallucinations, Dreams, and Hallucinations: The Framing Structure and its Representation in the Analytic Setting". In *The Greening of Psychoanalysis.* Edited by Rosine Jozef Perelberg and Gregorio Kohon. London: Karnac Books.

Perelberg, Rosine Jozef, and Gregorio Kohon, eds. 2017. *The Greening of Psychoanalysis.* London: Karnac Books.

Pontalis, Jean-Bertrand. 2000. "L'affirmation négative". *Libres Cahiers pour la Psychanalyse* 2 (2): 11–18.

Reed, Gail S., and Howard B. Levine, eds. 2018. *André Green Revisited: Representation and the Work of the Negative.* London: Routledge.

Reed, Gail S., and Rachel Boué Widawsky. 2018. "Green's Theory of Representation Revisited". In *André Green Revisited: Representation and the Work of the Negative.* Edited by Gail S. Reed and Howard B. Levine. London: Routledge.

Urribarri, Fernando, 2018. "The Negative and Its Vicissitudes: A New Contemporary Paradigm for Psychoanalysis". In *André Green Revisited: Representation and the Work of the Negative.* Edited by Gail S. Reed and Howard B. Levine. London: Routledge.

Index

For Product Safety Concerns and Information please contact our EU
representative GPSR@taylorandfrancis.com Taylor & Francis Verlag GmbH,
Kaufingerstraße 24, 80331 München, Germany

Printed and bound by CPI Group (UK) Ltd, Croydon, CR0 4YY
30/04/2026
02100338-0002